THE ULTIMATE NINJA FOODI GRILL COOKBOOK FOR BEGINNERS

1000 Days of Quick, Easy and Delicious Recipes for Everyday Indoor Grilling with Different Ninja Models!|Full Color Pictures Version

DEBORAH H. MOORE

Copyright© 2022 By Deborah H. Moore Rights Reserved

This book is copyright protected. It is only for personal use. You cannot amend, distribute, sell, use, quote or paraphrase any part of the content within this book, without the consent of the author or publisher.

Under no circumstances will any blame or legal responsibility be held against the publisher, or author, for any damages, reparation, or monetary loss due to the information contained within this book, either directly or indirectly.

Disclaimer Notice:

Please note the information contained within this document is for educational and entertainment purposes only. All effort has been executed to present accurate, up to date, reliable, complete information. No warranties of any kind are declared or implied. Readers acknowledge that the author is not engaged in the rendering of legal, financial, medical or professional advice. The content within this book has been derived from various sources. Please consult a licensed professional before attempting any techniques outlined in this book.

By reading this document, the reader agrees that under no circumstances is the author responsible for any losses, direct or indirect, that are incurred as a result of the use of the information contained within this document, including, but not limited to, errors, omissions, or inaccuracies.

Table of Contents

Introduction	**1**
Chapter 1	
Basics of Ninja Foodi Grill	**2**
Getting Familiar with the Functions	
Features of Ninja Foodi Grill	
Getting Familiar with the Functions	4
Features of Ninja Foodi Grill	5
Some Awesome Benefits Of Using An Electric Grill	6
Ninja Test Kitchen FAQ	7
Dos and Don'ts	8
The Perfect Temp	9
How to Clean and Maintain	10
Chapter 2	
Breakfast Recipes	**11**
Bistro Breakfast Sandwiches	12
Zesty Grilled Ham	12
Prosciutto Egg Panini	12
Roasted Garlic Potatoes	12
Scrambled Egg Bread	13
Eggs in Avocado cup	13
Breakfast Skewers	13
Breakfast Burger	14
Sausage with Eggs	14
Campfire Hash	14
Spinach Tater Tot Casserole	15
Grilled French Toast	15

Grilled Honeydew	15
Easy French Toast	16
Espresso Glazed Bagels	16
Chapter 3	
Poultry Recipes	**17**
Balinese Grilled Chicken	18
Grilled Chicken Wings with Jaew	18
Chicken Thigh Yakitori	18
Tomato Turkey Burgers	19
Grilled Chicken with Banana Pepper Dip	19
Peruvian Chicken Skewers	19
Kewpie-Marinated Chicken	20
Chicken Paillards with Fresh Tomato Sauce	20
Grilled Duck Breast	21
Grilled Wild Duck Breast	21
Super Barbeque Chicken	21
Greek Chicken with Tzatziki Sauce	22
Sriracha Wings	22
Grilled Chicken with Mustard Barbecue Sauce	22
Grilled Chicken Fajitas	23
Cheesy Chicken in Leek-Tomato Sauce	23
Balsamic-Rosemary Chicken Breasts	23
Mustard Chicken Tenders	24
Honey BBQ-Glazed Chicken Drumsticks	24
Baked Soy Chicken	25
Chicken Alfredo Apples	25

Chapter 4
Meat Recipes — 26
Mojo-Marinated Pork Kebabs	27
Grilled Pork Chops with Plums	27
Pork Tenderloin with Peach-Mustard Sauce	27
Ninja Foodi Grill Steak	28
Pork Cutlets with Cantaloupe Salad	28
Steak Kabobs	28
Grilled Pork Belly Kebabs	29
Grilled Pork Tenderloin Marinated in Spicy Soy Sauce	29
Garlic Butter Pork	29
Korean Pork	30
BBQ Beef Short Ribs	30
Curried Pork Skewers	30
Steak and Potatoes	31
Balinese Pork Satay	31
Pork with Salsa	31

Chapter 5
Seafood Recipes — 32
Grilled Ahi Tuna	33
Grilled Coconut and Pineapple Sweet Chili Shrimp	33
Grilled Calamari	33
Tuna Burgers	34
Grilled Scallops	34
Scallops with Creamed Corn	34
Shrimp Boil	35
Pineapple Shrimp Skewers	35
Grilled Oysters	35
Grilled Shrimp Tostadas with Guacamole	36
Shrimp and Chorizo Grill	36
Nigerian Skewers	37
Shrimp with Tomatoes	37

Chapter 6
Vegetarian Recipes — 38
Charred Asparagus Tacos	39
Eggplant Caprese	39
Cool Rosemary Potatoes	39
Tomato Salsa	40
Potatoes in a Foil	40
Veggie Kabobs	40
Delicious Broccoli and Arugula	41
Chinese Eggplant	41
Mustard Green Veggie Meal	41
Vegetable Orzo Salad	42
Southwestern Potato Salad	42
Cheddar Cauliflower Meal	43
Mushroom Tomato Roast	43
Grilled Brussels Sprouts with Bacon	44
Grilled Smashed Potatoes	44
Buttery Spinach Meal	45
Zucchini Rolls with Goat Cheese	45
Zucchini with Parmesan	46
Cheddar Bacon Corn	46
Apple Salad	47
Sweet Grilled Pickles	47

Chapter 7
Snack and Side Recipes — 48
Volcano Potatoes	49
Ginger Salmon	49
Crispy Rosemary Potatoes	49
Baked Banana	50
Pig Candy	50
Basil Shrimp Appetizer	50
Bison Sliders	50
Lovely Seasonal Broccoli	51
Mayonnaise Corn	51
Grilled Peach Salsa	51
Grilled Butternut Squash	51
Grilled Kimchi	52
Grilled Stuffed Mushrooms	52
Air Fryer Avocado Fries	52
Figs Stuffed with Cheese	53
Cob with Pepper Butter	53
Grilled Potato Wedges	53
Tarragon Asparagus	53

Chapter 8
Bonus — 54
Peach BBQ Chicken Thighs	55
Grilled Huli Huli Chicken	55
Beer Bratwurst	55
Chicken Roast with Pineapple Salsa	56
Grilled Chicken Bruschetta	56
Chicken & Bacon Caesar Salad	56
Orange Curried Chicken	57
Honey-Mustard Chicken Tenders	57
Air Fryer Chicken Fajitas	57
Chili-Spiced Ribs	57
Tarragon Chicken Tenders	58
Minted Tomato, Onion & Glazed Tofu Kebabs	58
Grilled Pork Chops with Pineapple Glaze	58
Marinated London Broil	59
Carne Asada Street Tacos	59
Juicy Stuffed Bell Peppers	59
Chicken Satay	60
Moroccan Roast Chicken	60

Appendix 1 Measurement Conversion Chart — 61
Appendix 2 The Dirty Dozen and Clean Fifteen — 62
Appendix 3 Index — 63

Introduction

Any indoor occasion is incomplete without tasty food. And what can be better than spicy grilled food? Grilling traditionally is a very hard job for many, it takes a lot of preparation. For a quick grilling solution, there is the Ninja Foodi grill. There are various kinds of grills in the market. The Ninja Foodi grill is one of the best grills to date. One might wonder why Ninja Foodi grill is the best out of all. Well, the answer is simple because it is more extensive, easy to navigate, has good burners, and is easy to clean. What other quality is required to be a good grill?

One of the hardest things about a grill is controlling its temperature which matters a lot. The ninja food grill's temperature is very easy to control and there is a timer for perfect cooking. Users just have to set the timer and temperature, the machine will do the rest of the job.

Chapter 1
Basics of Ninja Foodi Grill

Traditional grills are fire-powered and might burn the food in many positions and cause a bitter flavor. But the Ninja Foodi grill is hot air powered, cooks the food evenly from every side, and does not burn the food. Some might think it won't give that smokey flavor but that's not true. This grill will provide the spicy smoky flavor that everyone craves.

Grills get greasy and oily because of cooking non-veg food in them. Meats contain a lot of fat in them which causes oiliness. Manufacturers kept that in mind and designed the grill that way. The tray is easy to take out and clean.

Having a good grill does not mean the food will be good. The taste still depends on the cook and how he or she is cooking. As cooking in an electrical grill is different from cooking in traditional grills, the process might look hard. That is not true at all, with this cookbook in hand anyone can cook like a professional chef.

The best thing about this cookbook is it's not only about cooking but also has the answer to all questions related to a grill. From how to use, clean, and maintain. The users deserve justice and clarification. That's why this cookbook tells about both its pros and cons.

The grill does not come with a cookbook, so this cookbook is like a guardian angel to them. One can find nearly all kinds of recipes that they can cook on a grill. From starters to main courses and breakfast to lunch, every kind of recipe is in this book. The recipes are tested so one does not have to worry about their quality. This cookbook is perfect for everyone and people of every range. One can use it for themselves or as a gift to their old parents, close friends, and loved ones.

Feeding is the best way to express love towards someone, so express your love by cooking delicious meals and feeding them to your loved ones. Have a great day.

Getting Familiar with the Functions

GRILL

- This function involves searing stakes efficiently on the grill grate.
- The grill grate is of high density and provides effective grill marks with char-grilled flavors.
- The grill can accommodate a maximum of 6 fish fillets or burgers.

AIR CRISP

- The Air Crisp feature is based on the state-of-the-art air circulation used by Ninja Foodi in its devices.
- Rapid air circulation effectively uses hot air in air frying by cooking the food using circulated hot air.
- It uses around 80 percent less oil than traditional frying techniques.
- It requires a very limited quantity of oil for cooking.
- The food is also not soaked or immersed in large quantities of fatty oil, providing you effective health care as very little oil is used.
- The hot air is very efficient in air frying foods like chicken, fries, pastures, and fish, etc.

BROIL

- You can broil your food to give it a near-to-perfect crispy touch. We recommend you thoroughly check your food while you are broiling it to achieve more promising results.

BAKE & ROAST

- You can have better baking results while using the Ninja Foodi Smart XL Grill if you use the Ninja multi-purpose pan rather than the regular baking pan.
- You can also thoroughly put all your ingredients in the Crisper Basket for getting the perfect brownness of your food. It will provide you with an effective and thorough browning of the food evenly.
- You can also coat veggies with a little oil to have more crispiness and then air dry them to have more crispiness. We guarantee you that the final outcome will be truly matchless and delicious.

DEHYDRATE

- Always keep your ingredients dry before placing them in the Crisper Basket.
- It would be considered best if you did not stack or overlap the veggies in the basket. However, you can have more space by placing them closer and flat.
- Usually, fruits and veggies take around 6–8 hours to dehydrate properly. However, jerky takes 5–7 hours. To better understand dehydration, more dehydration means more crispiness in the final result. So for more crispiness, dehydrate the ingredients for a longer time.
- You can pasteurize ingredients by using the Roast Function at 300°F for one minute. It would be best if you do it before dehydrating fish and meat for more promising results.

Features of Ninja Foodi Grill

1. The unique Ninja Foodi Grill is Integrated Smart Probe. The grill sears, sizzles, and air fry crisps as well as mainly indoor grill and air fryer.

2. You can cook food with precision and quality and without generating smoke indoor.

3. The air circulates inside the Ninja Foodi grill of about 500F on all sides of the grill.

4. The 500F air circulates all around the food for amazing crispiness and searing while the high-density grill creates amazing char-grilled marks and lovely flavors to food.

5. The Ninja Foodi Grill allows awesome control of setting: Low, Medium, High, and Max.

6. The wide temperature range of 105F500F and variable fan speed enable 5 fast, and versatile cooking functions: Grill, Air Crisp, Dehydrate, Roast, and Bake.

7. Air fry crisp with up to 75% less fat than deep-frying, using the included 4-qt crisper basket

8. No need to cut into foods or constantly probe them like when using an instant-read thermometer. Thus, you can eliminate guesswork and never worry about under or overcooking with the Integrated Smart Probe. Multi-task with peace of mind as food cooks to perfection

9. Instinctive digital display lets you easily choose a cooking function and see your food's internal temperature as the Integrated Smart Probe monitors it. The grill will conveniently help you when your food is perfectly cooked

10. Virtually smoke-free with unique Smoke Control Technology. The combination of a temperature-controlled grill grate, splatter shield, and cool-air zone reduces smoke, keeping it out of the kitchen

Some Awesome Benefits Of Using An Electric Grill

IT GIVES YOUR FULL FREEDOM OVER COOKING

1. Even if you have an outdoor grill, there are times when you just might not feel like firing it up because it requires a significant amount of effort. Several different factors, such as weather, charcoal, and so on, need to be kept in check.

2. With an indoor grill such as the Ninja Smart XL Grill, you just need electricity, and you can grill any meal you want with ease.

VERY EASY AND STRAIGHTFORWARD TEMPERATURE CONTROLS

3. Unlike traditional outdoor Grill that requires very skilled eyes and hands to keep the temperature in check, the Ninja Smart XL Grill is equipped with a great smart thermometer that allows you to regulate the temperature with ease and without any hassle.

4. With this appliance, your food will never be undercooked or overcooked. All you have to do is just select the temperature and let it do its magic!

STRAIGHTFORWARD AND SIMPLE AND TO CLEAN.

5. Opposed to outdoor grills, cleaning the Ninja Smart XL Grill is pretty easy to clean. All of this appliance's cooking components are coated with ceramic, making it very easy to clean. The other accessories, such as the Air Crisp basket and heating screen, can be simply washed in a dishwasher.

VERY EASY AND SIMPLE TO USE.

6. Contrary to what some people might say, using the Ninja Smart XL Grill is actually extremely easy. It is possibly one of the most straightforward appliances to use. All you have to do with this is just select the temperature, let the appliance preheat, and wait until you hear a beep.

7. Once you hear the beep, add food and let it cook on its own!

8. Once done, the machine will automatically notify you.

9. While the appliance might be a little bit heavy, you can still easily carry it wherever you want, and it can be used as both an indoor or outdoor appliance.

Ninja Test Kitchen FAQ

Q: How long should I preheat?

A. Grill mode takes approximately 10 minutes to preheat. Air Crisp, Roast, and Bake take approximately 3 minutes to preheat. And the unit does not preheat in either Broil or Dehydrate modes.

Q: Can I put the accessories in the dishwasher?

A. The Cooking Pot, Grill Grate, Splatter Shield, and Crisper Basket are all dishwasher safe. The only exception is the Smart Thermometer, which should not go in the dishwasher.

Q: How do I clean the thermometer?

A. The thermometer should be handwashed only. To deep clean, soak the stainless steel tip and grip in warm, soapy water. Do not immerse the jack or cord in water or any other liquid.

Q: How would I clean the splatter shield?

A. It is recommended to clean the splatter shield after every use. Soaking it overnight will help soften the baked-on grease. After soaking, use the cleaning brush to remove grease from the stainless steel frame and front tabs.

Q: Can I cancel preheating?

A. Preheating is highly recommended but can be skipped by selecting the PREHEAT button after you press the START/STOP button.

Q: Should I add ingredients before or after preheating?
A. For best results, let the unit fully preheat before adding ingredients.

Dos and Don'ts

1. DO let the unit completely preheat before placing items on the unit for cooking. While the unit is preheating, you can prep and gather all your ingredients and tools needed for grilling.

2. DO use proper grilling tools and accessories. You do not want to use metal utensils or metal spatulas to remove or stir food around on the Grill Grate, as they can scratch and damage the nonstick surface.

3. DO clean the Splatter Shield after every use. The Splatter Shield is easily removable. It is a breeze to clean by soaking it in dish soap and hot water. For tougher, baked-on grease, you can use a leave-on oven cleaner spray.

4. DON'T cook on a dirty Grill Grate. Make sure all parts are clean for each new use. Reusing a dirty part can create smoke from burnt bits of food left behind.

5. DON'T spray your Grill Grate, Crisper Basket, or Cooking Pot with oil. There is no need to spray the parts, because they all have a nonstick ceramic coating. If you wish to use oil, it is best to add the oil to the food or use it in your marinade before cooking.

6. DON'T cook foods with wet batter when using the AIR CRISP function. The batter will run off, and you will end up with burnt glop in the basket. I suggest freezing batter-coated food first for best results, or instead of batter, use a classic egg wash, then coat with panko, plain, or seasoned bread crumbs.

The Perfect Temp

PROTEIN	COOK TO INTERNAL TEMP OF:	CARRY-OVER COOK TO INTERNAL TEMP OF:
Fish	140°F	145°F
Poultry	165°F	165°F or higher
Pork	140°F	145°F
Beef/Lamb (Rare)	120°F	125°F*
Beef/Lamb (Medium-Rare)	130°F	135°F*
Beef/Lamb (Medium)	140°F	145°F
Beef/Lamb (Medium-Well)	145°F	150°F
Beef/Lamb (Well)	155°F	160°F
Ground Beef	155°F	160°F or higher
Ground Pork	155°F	160°F
Ground Poultry	165°F	165°F or higher

How to Clean and Maintain

1. The unit should be cleaned thoroughly after every use.

2. Before cleaning, unplug the unit from the outlet.

3. **Never** put the cooker base in the dishwasher or submerge it in water or other liquid.

4. Wipe the cooker base and control panel clean with a clean damp cloth.

5. The dishwasher is safe for the cooking pot, silicone ring, reversible rack, Cook & Crisp Basket, and detachable diffuser.

6. Water and dish soap can be used to clean the pressure lid, including the pressure release valve and anti-clog cap. **Do not** use the dishwasher to clean the pressure lid or any of its components, and **do not** disassemble the pressure release valve or red float valve assembly.

7. After the heat shield has cooled, wipe down the crisping lid with a wet cloth or paper towel.

8. If there is food residue on the cooking pot, reversible rack, or Cook & Crisp Basket, fill it with water and soak it before cleaning. **Scouring pads should not be used**. Scrub with a non-abrasive cleanser or liquid dish soap and a nylon pad or brush if necessary.

9. After each use, air-dry all parts or use a soft dry towel.

Chapter 2
Breakfast Recipes

Bistro Breakfast Sandwiches

Prep time: 10 minutes | Cooking time: 12 minutes | Serves 2

- 2 tsp. butter
- 4 large eggs, beaten
- 4 hearty Italian bread slices
- ⅛ tsp. salt
- ⅛ tsp. black pepper
- 4 oz. smoked Gouda, cut in 4 slices
- 1 medium pear, sliced
- 4 strips of Canadian bacon, cooked and sliced
- ½ cup fresh baby spinach

1. Sauté eggs with 1 tsp. butter in a skillet on medium heat.
2. Spread the eggs on top of 2 bread slices.
3. Add black pepper, salt, cheese slices, pear slices, spinach and bacon on top of the egg.
4. Then place the other bread slices on top.
5. Select the "Grill" Mode, set the temperature to MAX.
6. Use the arrow keys on the display to select the time to 8 minutes.
7. Press the START/STOP button to initiate preheating.
8. Once preheated, place the sandwiches in the Ninja Foodi Smart XL Grill.
9. Flip the sandwiches once cooked halfway through.
10. Slice and serve warm.

PER SERVING

Calories 629 | Fat 33g | Sodium 1510mg | Carbs 44g | Fiber 3.9g | Sugar 3g | Protein 38g

Zesty Grilled Ham

Prep time: 15 minutes | Cooking time: 10 minutes | Serves 4

- ⅓ cup packed brown sugar
- 2 tbsp. prepared horseradish
- 4 tsp. lemon juice
- 1 (1 lb.) fully cooked bone-in ham steak

1. Boil brown sugar, lemon juice and horseradish in a small saucepan.
2. Soak the ham slices in this mixture and coat well.
3. Select the "Grill" Mode, set the temperature to MED.
4. Press the START/STOP button to initiate preheating.
5. Once preheated, place the ham in the Ninja Foodi Smart XL grill.
6. Cover the hood and allow the grill to cook.
7. Serve warm.

PER SERVING

Calories 180 | Fat 5g | Sodium 845mg | Carbs 20g | Fiber 0g | Sugar 3g | Protein 14g

Prosciutto Egg Panini

Prep time: 15 minutes | Cooking time: 15 minutes | Serves 4

- 3 large eggs
- 2 large egg whites
- 6 tbsp. fat-free milk
- 1 green onion, thinly sliced
- 1 tbsp. Dijon mustard
- 1 tbsp. maple syrup
- 8 slices sourdough bread
- 8 thin prosciutto slices
- ½ cup sharp cheddar cheese, shredded
- 8 tsp. butter

1. Sauté onion with butter in a skillet for 1 minute.
2. Beat eggs with egg whites, mustard, and maple in a bowl.
3. Pour this mixture into the skillet, stir and cook for 5 minutes.
4. Pour it over half of the bread slices.
5. Add ham, and cheddar cheese on top and place remaining bread slices on top.
6. Select the "Grill" Mode, set the temperature to MED.
7. Use the arrow keys to set the cooking time to 10 minutes.
8. Press the START/STOP button to initiate preheating.
9. Once preheated, place the sandwich in the Ninja Foodi Smart XL Grill.
10. Cover the hood and allow the grill to cook.
11. Flip the sandwiches once cooked halfway through.
12. Slice and serve warm.

PER SERVING

Calories 228 | Fat 10g | Sodium 640mg | Carbs 21g | Fiber 4g | Sugar 8g | Protein 13g

Roasted Garlic Potatoes

Prep time: 10 minutes | Cooking time: 20 minutes | Serves 6

- 2 lb. baby potatoes, sliced into wedges
- 2 tbsp. olive oil
- 2 tsp. garlic salt

1. Toss the potatoes in olive oil and garlic salt
2. Add the potatoes to the basket of the Ninja Foodi preheated. Close the lid
3. Set it to Air Fryer. Cook at 390°F for 20 minutes
4. Serve and Enjoy

PER SERVING

Calories: 131| Total Fat: 4.8g| Saturated Fat: 0.7g| Cholesterol: 0mg| Sodium: 15mg| Total Carbohydrate: 19.5g| Dietary Fiber: 3.9g| Total Sugars: 0.2g| Protein: 4.1g| Potassium: 635mg.

Scrambled Egg Bread
Prep time: 15 minutes|Cooking time: 14 minutes|Serves 4

- 1 loaf (1 lb.) sliced French bread
- 2 tbsp. butter, softened
- Filling:
- 2 tbsp. butter
- 1 small onion, chopped
- 1 cup cubed fully cooked ham
- 1 large tomato, chopped
- 6 large eggs
- ⅛ tsp. pepper
- 1-½ cups cheddar cheese, shredded

1. Cut the bread in half, crosswise then cut each half lengthwise.
2. Hollow 2 pieces of the cut bread to get ½ inch shells and dice the inner portion of the bread into cubes.
3. Toss the bread cubes with 1 tbsp. butter in a bowl.
4. Sauté onion with 1 tbsp. butter in a skillet for 4 minutes.
5. Stir in tomatoes and ham then mix well.
6. Beat eggs with pepper and remaining butter in a bowl.
7. Pour them over the ham mixture and add 1 cup cheese and bread cubes on top.
8. Cook this mixture for 5 minutes until the eggs are set.
9. Place the bread shells on a foil sheet and stuff each with egg mixture.
10. Add remaining cheese on top.
11. Select the "Bake" Mode, set the temperature to 350 degrees F.
12. Use the arrow keys on the display to select time to 4 minutes.
13. Press the START/STOP button to initiate preheating.
14. Cover the hood and let the appliance cook.
15. Serve warm.

PER SERVING

Calories 297 | Fat 15g |Sodium 548mg | Carbs 15g | Fiber 4g | Sugar 1g | Protein 19g

Eggs in Avocado cup
Prep time: 10 minutes|Cooking time: 12 minutes|Serves 2

- 1 avocado, halved and pitted
- Salt and ground black pepper, as required
- 2 eggs
- 1 tbsp. Parmesan cheese, shredded
- 1 tsp. fresh chives, minced

1. Arrange a greased square piece of foil on the basket.
2. Arrange the basket in the Ninja Foodi.
3. Close the Ninja Foodi and select "Bake/Roast."
4. Set the temperature to 390°F for 5 minutes.
5. Press "Start/Stop" to start preheating.
6. Carefully scoop out about 2 teaspoons of flesh from each avocado half.
7. Crack 1 egg in each avocado half and sprinkle with salt, black pepper and cheese.
8. After preheating, open the lid.
9. Place the avocado halves into the basket.
10. Close the Ninja Foodi lid and Select "Bake/Roast."
11. Set the temperature to 390°F for 12 minutes.
12. Press "Start/Stop" to start cooking.
13. Open the lid and transfer the avocado halves onto serving plates.
14. Top with Parmesan and chives and serve them.

PER SERVING

Calories: 278| Fat: 24.7g| Saturated Fat: 5.9g| Trans Fat: 18.8g| Carbohydrates: 9.1g| Fiber: 6.7g| Sodium: 188mg| Protein: 8.4g

Breakfast Skewers
Prep time: 15 minutes|Cooking time: 8 minutes|Serves 4

- 1 package (7 oz.) cooked sausage links, halved
- 1 can (20 oz.) pineapple chunks, drained
- 10 medium fresh mushrooms
- 2 tbsp. butter, melted
- Maple syrup

1. Toss sausages, pineapple, and mushrooms with butter and maple syrup in a bowl.
2. Thread these on the wooden skewers.
3. Select the "Grill" Mode, set the temperature to MED.
4. Use the arrow keys to set the cooking time to 8 minutes.
5. Press the START/STOP button to initiate preheating.
6. Once preheated, place the skewers in the Ninja Foodi Smart XL Grill.
7. Cover the hood and allow the grill to cook.
8. Flip the skewers once cooked halfway through.
9. Serve warm.

PER SERVING

Calories 246 | Fat 20g |Sodium 114mg | Carbs 13g | Fiber 1g | Sugar 10g | Protein 7g

Breakfast Burger

Prep time: 15 minutes | Cooking time: 26 minutes | Serves 4

- 1 lb. ground beef
- 1 tbsp. Worcestershire sauce
- 1 tsp. Montreal steak seasoning
- ½ tsp. salt
- ½ tsp. pepper
- 8 Texas toast slices
- 2 tbsp. canola oil
- 2-½ cups hash brown potatoes, shredded
- 4 American cheese slices
- 8 cooked bacon strips

1. Mix beef with ¼ tsp. black pepper, ¼ tsp. salt, steak seasoning and Worcestershire sauce in a bowl.
2. Make 4-½ inch thick patties out of this beef mixture.
3. Select the "Grill" Mode, set the temperature to MED.
4. Press the START/STOP button to initiate preheating.
5. Once preheated, place the patties in the Ninja Foodi Smart XL Grill.
6. Cover the hood and allow the grill to cook.
7. Transfer the patties to a plate.
8. Brush the toast slices with butter and grill them for 2 minutes from both the sides.
9. Similarly, grill the hash browns for 6 minutes per side.
10. Divide the patties, hash brown, cheese, and bacon strip in the grilled toasts.
11. Serve.

PER SERVING

Calories 859 | Fat 49g | Sodium 595mg | Carbs 55g | Fiber 6g | Sugar 13g | Protein 45g

Sausage with Eggs

Prep time: 15 minutes | Cooking time: 10 minutes | Serves 4

- 4 sausage links
- 2 cups kale, chopped
- 1 sweet yellow onion, chopped
- 4 eggs
- 1 cup mushrooms
- Olive oil

1. Place the cooking pot in the Ninja Foodi Smart XL Grill then place the grill grate in the pot.
2. Place the sausages in the Ninja Foodi Smart XL Grill.
3. Cover the Ninja Foodi Smart XL Grill's Hood, select the Grill mode, set the temperature to Low and grill for 2 minutes.
4. Flip the sausages and continue grilling for another 3 minutes
5. Now spread the onion, mushrooms, sausages, and kale in an iron skillet.
6. Crack the eggs in between the sausages.
7. BAKE this mixture for 5 minutes in the grill at 350 degrees F.
8. Serve warm and fresh.

PER SERVING

Calories 212 | Fat 12g | Sodium 321mg | Carbs 14.6g | Fiber 4g | Sugar 8g | Protein 17g

Campfire Hash

Prep time: 10 minutes | Cooking time: 31 minutes | Serves 4

- 1 large onion, chopped
- 2 tbsp. canola oil
- 2 garlic cloves, minced
- 4 large potatoes, peeled and cubed
- 1 lb. smoked kielbasa sausage, halved and sliced
- 1 can (4 oz.) green chiles, chopped
- 1 can (15-¼ oz.) whole kernel corn, drained

1. Sauté the onion with canola oil in a skillet for 5 minutes.
2. Stir in garlic and sauté for 1 minute then transfer to a baking pan.
3. Toss in potatoes and kielbasa then mix well.
4. Select the "Bake" Mode, set the temperature to 400 degrees F.
5. Use the arrow keys to set the cooking time to 20 minutes.
6. Press the START/STOP button to initiate preheating.
7. Once preheated, place the baking pan in the Ninja Foodi Smart XL Grill.
8. Cover the hood and allow the grill to cook.
9. Serve warm.

PER SERVING

Calories 535 | Fat 26g | Sodium 1097g | Carbs 46g | Fiber 4g | Sugar 8g | Protein 17g

The Ultimate Ninja Foodi Grill Cookbook for Beginners

Spinach Tater Tot Casserole

Prep time: 10 minutes | Cooking time: 8 minutes | Serves 8

- 8 eggs
- 15 ounces frozen tater tots
- 1½ cup cheddar cheese, shredded
- 4 ounces fresh spinach, chopped & sautéed
- 1 cup roasted red peppers, chopped
- Pepper
- Salt

1. In a bowl, whisk eggs with pepper and salt. Add cheese, roasted peppes and spinach, stir well.
2. Place the tater tots into the greased baking dish. Pour egg mixture over tater tots.
3. Inset the cooking pot and place your own baking dish in the pot. Select Bake mode, set the tempertaure to 350 degrees F and time to 40 minutes.
4. Press START/STOP to begin preheating.
5. Once preheated, place the food in, cover the hood and let the appliance grill.
6. Serve.

PER SERVING

Calories 254 | Fat 16g | Sodium 680mg | Carbs 15g | Fiber 1g | Sugar 680g | Protein 12g

Grilled French Toast

Prep time: 15 minutes | Cooking time: 8 minutes | Serves 6

- 3 eggs
- 1-quart strawberries, quartered
- 2 tablespoons aged Balsamic vinegar
- Juice of 1 orange and 2 teaspoons orange zest
- 1 sprig of fresh rosemary
- ¾ cup heavy cream
- 2 tablespoons honey
- 1 teaspoon vanilla extract
- Salt to taste
- 6 1-inch challah bread slices
- Fine sugar, for dusting

1. Place the cooking pot in the Ninja Foodi Smart XL Grill then place the grill grate in the pot.
2. Spread a foil sheet on a working surface.
3. Add strawberries, Balsamic, orange juice, rosemary and zest.
4. Fold the foil edges to make a pocket.
5. Whisk egg with cream, honey, vanilla and a pinch of salt.
6. Dip and soak the bread slices in this mixture and shake off the excess.
7. Select the "Grill" Mode, set the temperature to MED.
8. Press the START/STOP button to initiate preheating.
9. Place the bread slices and the foil packets in the Ninja Foodi Smart XL Grill.
10. Cover the hood and allow the grill to cook for 3 minutes.
11. Flip the bread slices and continue grilling for another 3 minutes.
12. Serve the bread with the strawberry mix.
13. Enjoy.

PER SERVING

Calories 387 | Fat 6g | Sodium 154mg | Carbs 37.4g | Fiber 2.9g | Sugar 15g | Protein 15g

Grilled Honeydew

Prep time: 15 minutes | Cooking time: 6 minutes | Serves 4

- ¼ cup peach preserves
- 1 tbsp. lemon juice
- 1 tbsp. crystallized ginger, chopped
- 2 tsp. lemon zest, grated
- ⅛ tsp. ground cloves
- 1 medium honeydew melon, cut into cubes

1. Mix peaches preserves with lemon juice, ginger, lemon zest, and cloves in a bowl.
2. Thread the honeydew melon on the wooden skewers.
3. Brush the prepared glaze over the skewers liberally.
4. Select the "Grill" Mode, set the temperature to MED.
5. Use the arrow keys to set the cooking time to 6 minutes.
6. Press the START/STOP button to initiate preheating.
7. Once preheated, place the skewers in the Ninja Foodi Smart XL Grill.
8. Cover the hood and allow the grill to cook.
9. Flip the skewers once cooked halfway through.
10. Serve.

PER SERVING

Calories 101 | Fat 0g | Sodium 18mg | Carbs 26g | Fiber 3.6g | Sugar 6g | Protein 1g

The Ultimate Ninja Foodi Grill Cookbook for Beginners

Easy French Toast

Prep time: 10 minutes | Cooking time: 8 minutes | Serves 3

- 3 1-inch slices challah bread
- 2 eggs
- Juice of ½ orange
- ½ quart strawberries, quartered
- 1 tbsp. honey
- 1 tbsp. balsamic vinegar
- 1 tsp. orange zest
- ½ sprig fresh rosemary
- ½ tsp. vanilla extract
- Salt to taste
- ¼ cup heavy cream
- Fine sugar, for dusting, optional

1. Spread a foil sheet on a working surface.
2. Add strawberries, balsamic vinegar, orange juice, rosemary and zest and fold the foil edges to make a pocket.
3. Whisk the egg with cream, honey, vanilla and a pinch of salt in a bowl.
4. Dip and soak the bread slices in this mixture and shake off the excess.
5. Prepare and preheat the Ninja Foodi Grill in a medium-temperature setting.
6. Once it is preheated, open the lid and place the bread slices and the foil packet on the grill.
7. Cover the Ninja Foodi Grill's lid and let them grill on the "Grilling Mode" for 2 minutes in batches.
8. Flip the bread slices and continue grilling for another 2 minutes.
9. Serve the bread with the strawberry mix on top.

PER SERVING

Calories: 387| Total Fat: 6g| Saturated Fat: 9.9g| Cholesterol: 41mg| Sodium: 154mg| Total Carbs: 37.4g| Fiber: 2.9g| Sugar: 15.3g| Protein: 14.6g

Espresso Glazed Bagels

Prep time: 10 minutes | Cooking time: 8 minutes | Serves 4

- 4 bagels split in half
- ¼ cup coconut milk
- 1 cup fine sugar
- 2 tbsp. black coffee
- 2 tbsp. coconut flakes

1. Prepare and preheat the Ninja Foodi Grill at a medium temperature setting.
2. Once it is preheated, open the lid and place 2 bagels in the grill.
3. Cover the Ninja Foodi Grill's lid and let it grill on the "Grilling Mode" for 2 minutes.
4. Flip the bagel and continue grilling for another 2 minutes.
5. Grill the remaining bagels in a similar way.
6. Whisk the rest of the in a bowl well.
7. Drizzle this sauce over the grilled bagels.
8. Serve and enjoy.

PER SERVING

Calories: 412| Total Fat: 24.8g| Saturated Fat: 12.4g| Cholesterol: 3mg| Sodium: 132mg| Total Carbs: 43.8g| Dietary Fiber: 3.9g| Sugar: 2.5g| Protein: 18.9g

Chapter 3
Poultry Recipes

Balinese Grilled Chicken

Prep time: 15 minutes|Cooking time: 10 minutes|Serves 6

- 3 tbsp. coconut oil
- 5 garlic cloves, smashed
- 2 tbsp. fresh makrut lime juice
- 1 tbsp. peeled fresh turmeric root, chopped
- 1 tbsp. peeled fresh ginger, chopped
- 1 tbsp. kosher salt
- 1 tsp. tamarind paste
- 1 tsp. ground coriander
- 3 lbs. chicken pieces

1. Place the cooking pot in the Ninja Foodi Smart XL Grill then set a grill grate inside.
2. Blend coconut oil and all other except chicken in a food processor.
3. Leave this mixture for 20 minutes then add the chicken and mix well.
4. Cover and marinate the chicken for 1 hour in the refrigerator.
5. Plug the thermometer into the appliance.
6. Select the "Grill" Mode, set the temperature to MED then select the PRESET.
7. Use the right arrow keys on the display to select "CHICKEN" and set the doneness to WELL.
8. Press the START/STOP button to initiate preheating.
9. Once preheated, place the chicken in the Ninja Foodi Smart XL Grill.
10. Insert the thermometer probe into the thickest part of the chicken.
11. Cover the hood and allow the grill to cook.
12. Serve warm.

PER SERVING

Calories 380 | Fat 19g |Sodium 318mg | Carbs 9g | Fiber 5g | Sugar 3g | Protein 26g

Grilled Chicken Wings with Jaew

Prep time: 15 minutes|Cooking time: 30 minutes|Serves 4

- Jaew
- ½ cup fish sauce
- 3 tbsp. fresh lime juice
- 2 tbsp. granulated sugar
- 2 tsp. red Thai chile powder
- 1 ½ tsp. toasted sesame seeds
- Wings
- ⅓ cup oyster sauce
- ¼ cup Thai seasoning sauce
- 2 tbsp. granulated sugar
- 2 tbsp. vegetable oil
- 1 ½ tsp. black pepper
- 30 chicken wing flats

1. Place the cooking pot in the Ninja Foodi Smart XL Grill then set a grill grate inside.
2. Mix chile powder, sugar, lime juice, and fish sauce in a bowl.
3. Stir in sesame seeds, and mix well then keep 3 tbsp. marinade aside.
4. Mix the remaining marinade with the chicken in a large bowl.
5. Cover and refrigerate for 30 minutes for marination.
6. Mix the reserved marinade and remaining in a bowl.
7. Thread the chicken on the wooden skewers and brush the prepared glaze over them.
8. Select the "Grill" Mode, set the temperature to MED.
9. Press the START/STOP button to initiate preheating.
10. Once preheated, place the chicken in the Ninja Foodi Smart XL Grill.
11. Cover the hood and cook for 10 to 15 minutes per side until golden brown and tender.
12. Serve warm.

PER SERVING

Calories 344 | Fat 13g |Sodium 216mg | Carbs 7g | Fiber 3g | Sugar 4g | Protein 31g

Chicken Thigh Yakitori

Prep time: 15 minutes|Cooking time: 10 minutes|Serves 4

- ⅓ cup mild tare sauce
- 3 tbsp. tamari
- 1 ½ tbsp. wasabi paste
- 4 skinless, boneless chicken thighs
- 3 scallions, cut into 1-inch lengths
- Olive oil
- Salt, to taste

1. Mix wasabi with tamari and tare sauce in a bowl.
2. Toss in chicken pieces and mix well to coat.
3. Thread these chicken pieces and scallions over the wooden skewers then drizzle oil and salt.
4. Place the cooking pot in the Ninja Foodi Smart XL Grill then set a grill grate inside.
5. Select the "Grill" Mode, set the temperature to MED.
6. Press the START/STOP button to initiate preheating.
7. Once preheated, place the chicken in the Ninja Foodi Smart XL Grill.
8. Cover the hood and allow the grill to cook for 5 minutes per side.
9. Serve warm.

PER SERVING

Calories 357 | Fat 12g |Sodium 48mg | Carbs 16g | Fiber 2g | Sugar 0g | Protein 24g

Tomato Turkey Burgers

Prep time: 15 minutes | Cooking time: 14 minutes | Serves 6

- 1 large red onion, chopped
- 6 Ciabatta rolls, sliced in half
- 1 cup (4 ounces) Feta cheese
- ⅔ cup sun-dried tomatoes, chopped
- ¼ teaspoon salt
- ¼ teaspoon black pepper
- 2 pounds lean ground turkey

1. Take all the ingredients for burgers in a bowl except the Ciabatta rolls.
2. Mix well and make six patties out of this turkey mixture.
3. Place the cooking pot in the Ninja Foodi Smart XL Grill then place the grill grate in the pot.
4. Plug the thermometer into the appliance.
5. Select the "Grill" Mode, set the temperature to MED then select the PRESET.
6. Use the right arrow keys on the display to select "CHICKEN" and set the doneness to WELL.
7. Press the START/STOP button to initiate preheating.
8. Place the 2 patties in the Ninja Foodi Smart XL Grill.
9. Insert the thermometer probe into the thickest part of the patties.
10. Cover the hood and allow the grill to cook for 7 minutes per side.
11. Grill the remaining patties in a similar way.
12. Serve with Ciabatta rolls.

PER SERVING

Calories 301 | Fat 16g | Sodium 412mg | Carbs 32g | Fiber 0.2g | Sugar 1g | Protein 28.2g

Grilled Chicken with Banana Pepper Dip

Prep time: 15 minutes | Cooking time: 28 minutes | Serves 6

- 3 tbsp. olive oil
- 2 medium banana peppers sliced
- 4 oz. feta cheese, crumbled
- 3 tsp. fresh lemon juice
- ½ tsp. kosher salt
- ¼ tsp. black pepper
- 1 oz. pita bread
- 1 (6-oz.) boneless chicken breast
- 4 grape tomatoes, halved
- 1 small Persian cucumber, halved
- 1 tbsp. red onion, chopped
- 5 pitted kalamata olives, halved
- 2 tsp. torn fresh mint

1. Sauté banana peppers with 1 tbsp. oil in a skillet for 6 minutes.
2. Allow them to cool then blend with 2 tbsp. lemon juice in a blender until smooth.
3. Stir in black pepper and salt then mix well.
4. Rub the chicken with black pepper, salt and oil.
5. Place the cooking pot in the Ninja Foodi Smart XL Grill then set a grill grate inside.
6. Plug the thermometer into the appliance.
7. Select the "Grill" Mode, set the temperature to MED then select the PRESET.
8. Use the right arrow keys on the display to select "CHICKEN" and set the doneness to WELL.
9. Press the START/STOP button to initiate preheating.
10. Once preheated, place the chicken in the Ninja Foodi Smart XL Grill.
11. Insert the thermometer probe into the thickest part of the chicken.
12. Cover the hood and allow the grill to cook.
13. Transfer the chicken to a plate and cook the pita for 4 minutes per side.
14. Mix tomatoes with other in a bowl.
15. Slice the chicken and serve with banana pepper dip, pita and tomato mixture.
16. Serve.

PER SERVING

Calories 348 | Fat 12g | Sodium 710mg | Carbs 24g | Fiber 5g | Sugar 3g | Protein 34g

Peruvian Chicken Skewers

Prep time: 15 minutes | Cooking time: 10 minutes | Serves 4

- ½ cup ají panca paste
- 5 tbsp. olive oil
- 3 tbsp. red wine vinegar
- 2 tbsp. gochujang
- 1 tbsp. tamari or soy sauce
- 1 ½ tsp. toasted cumin seeds
- ¼ tsp. dried Mexican oregano
- ⅛ tsp. black pepper
- 1 large garlic clove
- 1 ½ lbs. boneless chicken thighs, cut into cubes
- huacatay Dipping Sauce

1. Mix chicken cubes with gochujang and other in a bowl.
2. Cover and refrigerate for 30 minutes then thread the chicken on the wooden skewers.
3. Place the cooking pot in the Ninja Foodi Smart XL Grill then set a grill grate inside.
4. Select the "Grill" Mode, set the temperature to MED.
5. Press the START/STOP button to initiate preheating.
6. Once preheated, place the chicken in the Ninja Foodi Smart XL Grill.
7. Cover the hood and allow the grill to cook for 10 minutes, flipping halfway through.
8. Serve warm with dipping sauce.

PER SERVING

Calories 329 | Fat 5g | Sodium 510mg | Carbs 17g | Fiber 5g | Sugar 4g | Protein 21g

Kewpie-Marinated Chicken

Prep time: 15 minute|Cooking time: 25 minutes|Serves 6

- 1 cup Kewpie mayonnaise
- 2 tsp. lime zest
- 1 ½ tbsp. ground cumin
- 1 ½ tbsp. hot paprika
- Kosher salt
- Black pepper
- Two 3-lb. whole chickens, cut into pieces
- olive oil, for brushing

1. Mix mayonnaise with 1 tsp. black pepper, 1 tbsp. salt, paprika, cumin and lime juice and zest.
2. Remove the chicken bones and flatten the meat with a mallet.
3. Cut slits over the chicken and place in a tray.
4. Spread and rub the prepared marinade over the chicken.
5. Cover and refrigerate for 2 hours.
6. Place the cooking pot in the Ninja Foodi Smart XL Grill then set a grill grate inside.
7. Plug the thermometer into the appliance.
8. Select the "Grill" Mode, set the temperature to MED then select the PRESET.
9. Use the right arrow keys on the display to select "CHICKEN" and set the doneness to WELL.
10. Press the START/STOP button to initiate preheating.
11. Once preheated, place the chicken in the Ninja Foodi Smart XL Grill.
12. Insert the thermometer probe into the thickest part of the chicken.
13. Cover the hood and allow the grill to cook.
14. Serve warm.

PER SERVING

Calories 375 | Fat 16g | Sodium 255mg | Carbs 4.1g | Fiber 1.2g | Sugar 5g | Protein 24.1g

Chicken Paillards with Fresh Tomato Sauce

Prep time: 8 minutes| Cooking time: 25 minutes|Serves 4

- 2 whole skinless, boneless chicken breasts (each 12 to 16 oz.), or 4 half breasts (each half 6 to 8 oz.)
- 1 garlic clove, minced
- 3 fresh basil leaves, minced, plus 4 basil sprigs for garnish
- Coarse salt (kosher or sea and freshly ground black pepper
- 2 tbsp. extra-virgin olive oil
- Tomato Sauce:
- 1 clove garlic, minced
- ½ tsp. salt, or more to taste
- 2 large ripe red tomato
- 12 niçoise olives, or 6 black olives, pitted and cut into ¼-inch dice
- 8 fresh basil leaves, thinly slivered
- ¼ cup extra-virgin olive oil
- 1 tbsp. red wine vinegar, or more to taste
- Freshly ground black pepper

1. If using whole chicken breasts, divide them in half.
2. Trim any sinews or excess fat off the chicken breasts and discard them.
3. Remove the tenders from the breasts and set them aside.
4. Rinse the breasts under cold running water; then drain them.
5. Place a breast half between 2 pieces of plastic wrap and gently pound it to a thickness of between ¼ and 1/8 inch using a meat pounder, the side of a heavy cleaver, a rolling pin, or the bottom of a heavy saucepan.
6. Repeat with the remaining breast halves.
7. Place the garlic and minced basil, ½ teaspoon of salt and ½ teaspoon of pepper in a bowl and mash to a paste with the back of a spoon.
8. Stir in the olive oil. Brush each paillard on both sides with the garlic and basil mixture and season lightly with salt and pepper.
9. Insert the Grill Grate and close the lid. Select GRILL, set the temperature to HIGH and set the time to 4 minutes.
10. Select START/STOP to start preheating.
11. Meanwhile, prepare the sauce.
12. Cut the tomatoes in half and squeeze them to get the pulp.
13. Put the pulp in a pan on high heat and add the other ingredients listed above (sauce ingredient list) and bring it to a boil.
14. Then lower the heat and simmer. Stir occasionally and let it reduce to the right density. Salt to taste.
15. The Ninja Foodi is preheated and ready to cook when it starts beeping.
16. Arrange the chicken on the grill and cook for 15 minutes.
17. Serve them warm.

PER SERVING

Calories: 299| Fat: 20g| Protein: 52g

Grilled Duck Breast

Prep time: 15 minutes|Cooking time: 10 minutes|Serves 4

- 4 large duck or small goose breasts, sliced
- Salt, to taste
- Olive or vegetable oil
- Black pepper, to taste

1. Season the duck breasts with black pepper, salt and oil.
2. Place the cooking pot in the Ninja Foodi Smart XL Grill then set a grill grate inside.
3. Plug the thermometer into the appliance.
4. Select the "Grill" Mode, set the temperature to MED then select the PRESET.
5. Use the right arrow keys on the display to select "CHICKEN" and set the doneness to WELL.
6. Press the START/STOP button to initiate preheating.
7. Once preheated, place the chicken in the Ninja Foodi Smart XL Grill.
8. Insert the thermometer probe into the thickest part of the duck.
9. Cover the hood and allow the grill to cook.
10. Serve warm.

PER SERVING

Calories 278 | Fat 4g |Sodium 232mg | Carbs 14g | Fiber 1g | Sugar 0g | Protein 21g

Grilled Wild Duck Breast

Prep time: 15 minutes|Cooking time: 10 minutes|Serves 8

- ¼ cup Worcestershire sauce
- 2 tbsp. olive oil
- ½ tsp. hot sauce
- 2 tbsp. garlic, minced
- ¼ tsp. black pepper
- 8 boned duck breast halves

1. Place duck breasts in a tray.
2. Mix oil and rest of the together and then pour over the duck.
3. Rub well and cover to refrigerate for 30 minutes.
4. Place the cooking pot in the Ninja Foodi Smart XL Grill then set a grill grate inside.
5. Plug the thermometer into the appliance.
6. Select the "Grill" Mode, set the temperature to MED then select the PRESET.
7. Use the right arrow keys on the display to select "CHICKEN" and set the doneness to WELL.
8. Press the START/STOP button to initiate preheating.
9. Once preheated, place the chicken in the Ninja Foodi Smart XL Grill.
10. Insert the thermometer probe into the thickest part of the duck.
11. Cover the hood and allow the grill to cook.
12. Serve warm.

PER SERVING

Calories 297 | Fat 25g |Sodium 122mg | Carbs 23g | Fiber 0.4g | Sugar 1g | Protein 43g

Super Barbeque Chicken

Prep time: 5-10 minutes|Cooking time: 12 minutes|Serves 3-4

- 6 chicken drumsticks
- 2 tsp. BBQ seasoning
- 1 pinch tsp. salt
- ½ cup ketchup
- 1 tbsp. brown sugar
- 1 tbsp. bourbon
- 1 tsp. dried onion, chopped finely
- ½ tbsp. Worcestershire sauce
- 1/3 cup spice seasoning

1. Stir-cook all the , except the drumsticks, for 8-10 minutes in a saucepan.
2. Set aside to cool down.
3. Take the Ninja Foodi Grill, arrange it over your kitchen platform and open the top lid.
4. Arrange the grill grate and close the top lid.
5. Press "GRILL" and select the "MED" grill function. Adjust the timer to 12 minutes and then press "START/STOP." Ninja Foodi will start preheating.
6. The Ninja Foodi is preheated and ready to cook when it starts beeping. After you hear a beep, open the top lid.
7. Arrange the drumsticks over the grill grate, brush with the sauce and cook it.
8. Serve them and enjoy.

PER SERVING

Calories: 342| Fat: 8.5g| Saturated Fat: 1g| Trans Fat: 0g| Carbohydrates: 10g| Fiber: 1.5g| Sodium: 319mg| Protein: 12.5g

Greek Chicken with Tzatziki Sauce

Prep time: 10 minutes | Cooking time: 15 minutes | Serves 4

- For the grilled chicken breasts:
- 4 chicken breasts
- ¼ cup extra-virgin olive oil
- 2 tsp dried oregano
- 1 tsp garlic powder
- Juice of one medium lemon
- Sea salt and freshly cracked pepper to taste
- For the tzatziki sauce:
- ½ cup finely grated cucumber
- 1 cup of Greek yogurt
- 2 tsp of apple cider vinegar
- Juice of one medium lemon
- 1 tbsp of garlic powder

1. For the chicken marinade, whisk together the lemon juice, olive oil, oregano, salt, pepper, and garlic powder in a medium bowl.
2. Pour into a Ziploc bag or container with the chicken to marinate in the refrigerator for at least 2 hours.
3. Meanwhile, make the tzatziki sauce by first grating the cucumbers.
4. Add in the Greek yogurt, vinegar, garlic, lemon juice, and sea salt to taste in a bowl. Chill in the refrigerator until ready to serve.
5. Select the "GRILL" function and adjust temperature to "HI", set the time to 15 minutes and preheat your Ninja Foodi Grill.
6. Add the marinated chicken.
7. Cook the chicken breasts for about 5-7 minutes per side, depending on thickness. Remove from grill and allow the cooked chicken to rest.

PER SERVING

Calories 521 | Carbohydrates 26g | Protein 59g | Fat 20g | Sodium 448mg | Fiber 2g

Sriracha Wings

Prep time: 15 minutes | Cooking time: 25 minutes | Serves 6

- 12 chicken wings
- 1 tablespoon canola oil
- 2 teaspoons ground coriander
- ½ teaspoon garlic salt
- ¼ teaspoon black pepper
- Glaze:
- ½ cup orange juice
- ⅓ cup Sriracha chili sauce
- ¼ cup butter, cubed
- 3 tablespoons honey
- 2 tablespoons lime juice
- ¼ cup fresh cilantro, chopped

1. Season the wings with all their seasoning in a suitable bowl.
2. Mix well, then cover to refrigerate for 2 hours of marination.
3. Meanwhile, prepare the sauce by cooking its in a saucepan for 4 minutes.
4. Place the cooking pot in the Ninja Foodi Smart XL Grill then place the grill grate in the pot.
5. Select the "Grill" Mode, set the temperature to MED.
6. Press the START/STOP button to initiate preheating.
7. Place the chicken wings in the Ninja Foodi Smart XL Grill.
8. Cover the hood and allow the grill to cook for 15 minutes.
9. Flip the grilled wings and continue cooking for another 10 minutes.
10. Drizzle the prepared sauce over the wings in a bowl.
11. Toss well and serve.

PER SERVING

Calories 352 | Fat 2.4g | Sodium 216mg | Carbs 16g | Fiber 2.3g | Sugar 1.2g | Protein 27g

Grilled Chicken with Mustard Barbecue Sauce

Prep time: 15 minutes | Cooking time: 20 minutes | Serves 4

- 2 tbsp. olive oil
- ¼ cup apple cider vinegar
- ¼ cup light brown sugar
- 2 tbsp. honey
- 2 tsp. Worcestershire sauce
- 1 tsp. garlic powder
- 1 tsp. paprika
- ¼ tsp. cayenne pepper
- ½ cup 2 tbsp. mustard
- 6 lb. bone-in chicken breasts
- Kosher salt
- 2 large sweet onions, sliced
- 1 (15-oz.) jar pickled green beans
- 2 lb. tomatoes, sliced into rounds

1. Mix the oil, vinegar, sugar, honey, Worcestershire sause, garlic powder, paprika, cayenne, and ½ cup mustard in a bowl.
2. Rub the chicken with 2 tbsp. salt.
3. Place the cooking pot in the Ninja Foodi Smart XL Grill then set a grill grate inside.
4. Select the "Grill" Mode, set the temperature to MED.
5. Once preheated, place the chicken in the Ninja Foodi Smart XL Grill.
6. Cover the hood and allow the grill to cook for 10 minutes per side.
7. Meanwhile, mix rest of the tomato salad (mustard, onions, green beans and tomatoes) in a bowl.
8. Serve the grilled chicken with this salad.
9. Enjoy.

PER SERVING

Calories 401 | Fat 7g | Sodium 269mg | Carbs 25g | Fiber 4g | Sugar 12g | Protein 26g

Grilled Chicken Fajitas

Prep time: 5 minutes|Cooking time: 8 minutes|Serves 6

- Chicken:
- ¼ cup olive oil, divided
- Juice from 1 lime
- 3 large boneless skinless chicken breasts, butterflied
- 1 each red, yellow, and orange peppers
- 1 medium Vidalia onion
- A pinch of salt
- 12 small soft flour tortillas
- Seasoning:
- 1½ tbsp. chili powder
- 2 tsp. ground cumin
- 2 tsp. kosher salt
- 2 tsp. smoked paprika
- 1 tsp. ground cinnamon
- 1 tsp. onion powder
- 1 tsp. garlic powder
- 1 tsp. cayenne pepper
- ½ tsp. white sugar
- Zest from 1 lime

1. Insert the Grill Grate and close the lid. Select GRILL, set the temperature to HIGH and set the time to 8 minutes. Select START/STOP to start preheating.
2. Combine all the seasoning into a small bowl and whisk together.
3. Whisk 2 tablespoons of olive oil and the lime juice together in a medium mixing bowl. Add butterflied chicken breasts. Toss to evenly coat.
4. Evenly sprinkle seasoning on both sides of the chicken, ensuring uniform coverage.
5. Thinly slice peppers and onion.
6. In a large mixing bowl, toss sliced vegetables with the remaining 2 tablespoons of olive oil and a pinch of salt.
7. The Ninja Foodi is preheated and ready to cook when it starts beeping. After you hear a beep, open the top lid.
8. Arrange the chicken over the grill grate and cook it.
9. Serve with sliced vegetables and enjoy.

PER SERVING

Calories 299| Fat: 20g| Protein: 52g

Cheesy Chicken in Leek-Tomato Sauce

Prep time: 10 minutes|Cooking time: 15 minutes|Serves 4

- 2 large-sized chicken breasts, cut in half lengthwise
- Salt and ground black pepper, to taste
- 4 oz. Cheddar cheese, cut into sticks
- 1 tbsp. sesame oil
- 1 cup leeks, chopped
- 2 cloves garlic, minced
- 2/3 cup tomato puree
- 1 tsp. dried rosemary
- 1 tsp. dried thyme

1. Insert the basket and close the lid.
2. Select AIR FRYER, set the temperature to 390°F and the time to 15 minutes.
3. Select START/STOP to start preheating.
4. Season the chicken breasts with salt and black pepper; place a piece of Cheddar cheese in the middle.
5. Then, tie it using a kitchen string. Drizzle with sesame oil and reserve.
6. Add the leeks, rosemary, thyme and garlic to the bowl.
7. Then arrange the chicken over the Air Fryer and cook it.
8. Serve it with tomato puree.

PER SERVING

Calories: 299| Fat: 20g| Protein: 52g

Balsamic-Rosemary Chicken Breasts

Prep time: 5 minutes |Cooking time: 6 minutes|Serves 4

- ½ cup balsamic vinegar
- 2 tbsp. olive oil
- 2 rosemary sprigs, coarsely chopped
- 2 lb. boneless, skinless chicken breasts, pounded to the ½-inch thickness

1. Combine the balsamic vinegar, olive oil and rosemary in a shallow baking dish.
2. Add the chicken breasts and turn to coat.
3. Cover with plastic wrap and refrigerate for at least 30 minutes or overnight.
4. Insert the Grill Grate and close the hood. Select GRILL, set the temperature to HIGH and set the time to 6 minutes.
5. Select START/STOP to start preheating.
6. When the unit beeps to indicate it has preheated, place the chicken breasts on the Grill Grate.
7. Close the lid and cook for 6 minutes until they get grill marks and are cooked through.
8. Serve them and enjoy.

PER SERVING

Calories: 299| Fat: 20g| Protein: 52g

Mustard Chicken Tenders

Prep time: 5 minutes | Cooking time: 20 minutes | Serves 4

- ½ cup coconut flour
- 1 tbsp. spicy brown mustard
- 2 beaten eggs
- 1 lb. chicken tenders
- Salt and pepper to taste

1. Insert the basket and close the lid.
2. Select AIR FRYER, set the temperature to 390°F and the time to 20 minutes.
3. Select START/STOP to start preheating.
4. Season the tenders with pepper and salt.
5. Place a thin layer of mustard onto the tenders and then dredge in flour and dip in egg.
6. Cook it and serve.

PER SERVING

Calories: 404| Fat: 20g| Protein: 22g| Sugar: 4g

Honey BBQ-Glazed Chicken Drumsticks

Prep time: 5 minutes | Cooking time: 45 minutes | Serves 5

- 10 to 12 chicken legs
- 2 tbsp. baking powder
- ½ tbsp. kosher salt
- Olive oil spray
- BBQ sauce
- 3 tbsp. honey

1. Remove the chicken from its packaging. Rinse and pat dry with a paper towel.
2. Mix baking powder and salt in a shaker bottle and dust over the drumsticks. Make sure you coat the skin lightly and evenly; this is essential to dry out the skin, which will allow for the skin to get crispy on the grill.
3. Place the chicken in the refrigerator for at least 1 to 2 hours to allow the baking powder and salt to pull the moisture out of the skin.
4. Mix together BBQ sauce and honey, generously coat both sides of the chicken drumsticks with sauce.
5. Insert the Grill Grate and close the hood. Select GRILL. Set the temperature to HIGH and the time to 45 minutes. Select START/STOP to start preheating.
6. Arrange the chicken over the grill and cook it.
7. Serve it and enjoy.

PER SERVING

Calories: 299| Fat: 20g| Protein: 52g

Baked Soy Chicken

Prep time: 5-10 minutes | Cooking time: 25 minutes | Serves 5-6

- ½ cup soy sauce
- ¼ cup apple cider vinegar
- 1 clove garlic, minced
- 1 tbsp. cornstarch
- 1 tbsp. cold water
- ½ cup white sugar
- ¼ tsp. ground black pepper
- ½ tsp. ground ginger
- 12 skinless chicken thighs
- Salt to taste

1. In a mixing bowl, add the cornstarch, water, white sugar, soy sauce, apple cider vinegar, garlic, ginger and black pepper. Combine the to mix well with each other.
2. Season the chicken with salt and ground black pepper.
3. Take a pan and lightly grease it with some cooking oil. In the pan, add the chicken and the soy mixture on top.
4. Take the Ninja Foodi Grill, arrange it over your kitchen platform and open the top lid.
5. Press "BAKE" and adjust the temperature to 350°F. Adjust the timer to 25 minutes and then press "START/STOP." Ninja Foodi will start preheating.
6. The Ninja Foodi is preheated and ready to cook when it starts beeping. After you hear a beep, open the top lid.
7. Arrange the pan directly inside the unit after brushing it with the sauce prepared earlier.
8. Close the top lid and allow it to cook until the timer reads zero.
9. Serve warm.

PER SERVING

Calories: 573| Fat: 19g| Saturated Fat: 5g| Trans Fat: 0g| Carbohydrates: 23.5g| Fiber: 1g| Sodium: 624mg| Protein: 48.5g

Chicken Alfredo Apples

Prep time: 5-10 minutes | Cooking time: 20 minutes | Serves 4

- 1 large apple, wedged
- 1 tbsp. lemon juice
- 4 chicken breasts, halved
- 4 tsp. chicken seasoning
- 4 slices provolone cheese
- ¼ cup blue cheese, crumbled
- ½ cup Alfredo sauce

1. Season the chicken in a bowl with chicken seasoning. In another bowl, toss the apple with lemon juice.
2. Take the Ninja Grill, arrange it over your kitchen platform and open the top lid.
3. Arrange the grill grate and close the top lid.
4. Press "GRILL" and select the "MED" grill function. Adjust the timer to 16 minutes and then press "START/STOP." The Ninja will start preheating.
5. The Ninja is preheated and ready to cook when it starts beeping. After you hear a beep, open the top lid.
6. Arrange the chicken over the grill grate.
7. Close the top lid and cook for 8 minutes. Now open the top lid, flip the chicken.
8. Close the top lid and cook for 8 more minutes.
9. Then, grill the apple in the same way for 2 minutes per side.
10. Serve the chicken with the apple, blue cheese and Alfredo sauce.

PER SERVING

Calories: 247| Fat: 19g| Saturated Fat: 3g| Trans Fat: 0g| Carbohydrates: 29.5g| Fiber: 2g| Sodium: 853mg| Protein: 14.5g

Chapter 4
Meat Recipes

Mojo-Marinated Pork Kebabs
Prep time: 15 minutes | Cooking time: 10 minutes | Serves 4

- Brined Pork:
- 2 quarts ice-cold water
- ⅓ cup kosher salt
- 1/4 cup sugar
- 2 lbs. center-cut pork chops
- Mojo Marinade
- 2 tbsp. garlic, minced
- ½ tsp. kosher salt
- ½ cup fresh sour orange juice
- ¼ cup olive oil
- ½ tsp. dried oregano
- ½ tsp. cumin
- Black pepper, to taste
- Skewers:
- 2 whole mangos, peeled, cored, and cut into 1 ½ -inch squares

1. Mix salt, sugar and water in a large pan and soak the pork for 1 hour.
2. Mash garlic, with ½ tsp. salt, cumin, oregano, oil, and orange juice in a mortar.
3. Remove the pork from the brine and cut into cubes.
4. Mix the pork with the marinade in a bowl, cover and refrigerate for 1 hour.
5. Thread the pork and mango cubes on the wooden skewers.
6. Place the cooking pot in the Ninja Foodi Smart XL Grill then set a grill grate inside.
7. Select the "Grill" Mode, set the temperature to MED.
8. Press the START/STOP button to initiate preheating.
9. Once preheated, place the pork in the Ninja Foodi Smart XL Grill.
10. Cover the hood and allow the grill to cook for 10 minutes, flipping halfway through.
11. Serve warm.

PER SERVING

Calories 425 | Fat 15g | Sodium 345mg | Carbs 23g | Fiber 1.4g | Sugar 3g | Protein 33.3g

Grilled Pork Chops with Plums
Prep time: 15 minutes | Cooking time: 12 minutes | Serves 4

- 4 tbsp. olive oil
- 1 tsp. honey
- 4 bone-in pork rib chops (1" thick), patted dry
- Kosher salt and ground pepper, to taste
- 4 ripe medium plums, halved
- 1 lemon, halved, seeds removed
- 8 oz. Halloumi cheese, sliced
- 2 tbsp. torn oregano leaves
- Aleppo-style pepper flakes, for serving

1. Season the pork chops with black peppers, salt, 2 tbsp. oil and honey.
2. Toss plums with lemon, halloumi, salt, black pepper and 2 tbsp. oil in a bowl.
3. Place the cooking pot in the Ninja Foodi Smart XL Grill then set a grill grate inside.
4. Select the "Grill" Mode, set the temperature to MED.
5. Press the START/STOP button to initiate preheating.
6. Once preheated, place the pork in the Ninja Foodi Smart XL Grill.
7. Cover the hood and allow the grill to cook for 8 minutes, flipping halfway through.
8. Slice the pork chops and serve with grilled halloumi, plums and lemon.
9. Garnish with oregano, and peppers.
10. Enjoy.

PER SERVING

Calories 361 | Fat 16g | Sodium 189mg | Carbs 13g | Fiber 0.3g | Sugar 18.2g | Protein 33.3g

Pork Tenderloin with Peach-Mustard Sauce
Prep time: 11 minutes | Cooking time: 12 minutes | Serves 4

- Peach-Mustard Sauce:
- 2 large ripe peaches, peeled, diced
- ¼ cup ketchup
- 3 tbsp. Dijon mustard
- 1 tsp. light brown sugar
- ½ tsp. black pepper
- ½ tsp. kosher salt
- Pork:
- 2 pork tenderloins
- 4 tsp. kosher salt
- 1 tsp. black pepper
- Vegetable oil, for grill
- ½ cup peach preserves

1. Blend peaches with ½ tsp. salt, black pepper, brown sugar, mustard and ketchup in a blender.
2. Place the cooking pot in the Ninja Foodi Smart XL Grill then set a grill grate inside.
3. Plug the thermometer into the appliance.
4. Select the "Grill" Mode, set the temperature to MED then select the PRESET.
5. Use the right arrow keys on the display to select "PORK" and set the doneness to MED WELL.
6. Press the START/STOP button to initiate preheating.
7. Once preheated, place the pork in the Ninja Foodi Smart XL Grill.
8. Insert the thermometer probe into the thickest part of the pork.
9. Cover the hood and allow the grill to cook.
10. Slice the pork and serve with peach sauce.

PER SERVING

Calories 445 | Fat 7.9g | Sodium 581mg | Carbs 14g | Fiber 2.6g | Sugar 0.1g | Protein 42.5g

Ninja Foodi Grill Steak

Prep time: 5 minutes | Cooking time: 7 minutes | Serves 2

- 2 steaks
- 1 tbsp kosher salt
- ¼ tsp corn starch
- ½ tsp chili powder
- 2 tsp brown sugar
- ¼ tsp onion powder
- 1 tsp black pepper
- ¼ tsp Turmeric
- ½ tsp smoked paprika

1. Mix up all steak seasonings in a bowl.
2. Once steaks are rubbed down with the spices on all sides, wrap or cover and store in the fridge. Store for 30 minutes to 2 hours.
3. Select GRILL mode, set the temperature to MAX and time to 8-12 minutes. Press START/STOP to preheat the Ninja Foodi Grill.
4. Once the preheat is done take your steaks and place them on the grill.
5. You will cook your steaks to the doneness you desire.
6. Once steaks are done, allow resting on a plate for 5 minutes that is tented in aluminum foil.

PER SERVING

Calories 319 | Carbohydrates 3g | Protein 29g | Fat 21g | Sodium 1654mg | Fiber 0g

Pork Cutlets with Cantaloupe Salad

Prep time: 15 minutes | Cooking time: 8 minutes | Serves 4

- 4 (½-inch-thick) pork cutlets
- Kosher salt, to taste
- 1 cup grated cantaloupe
- 4 tbsp. fresh lime juice
- 2 tbsp. olive oil
- 4 scallions, sliced
- 1 red chile, sliced
- ¼ cup cilantro, chopped
- 2 tbsp. fish sauce
- Crushed salted, roasted peanuts

1. Prick the pork with a fork and season with 2 tbsp. lime juice, and cantaloupe in a bowl.
2. Cover and refrigerate for 1 hour.
3. Place the cooking pot in the Ninja Foodi Smart XL Grill then set a grill grate inside.
4. Plug the thermometer into the appliance.
5. Select the "Grill" Mode, set the temperature to MED then select the PRESET.
6. Use the right arrow keys on the display to select "PORK" and set the doneness to MED WELL.
7. Press the START/STOP button to initiate preheating.
8. Once preheated, place the pork in the Ninja Foodi Smart XL Grill.
9. Insert the thermometer probe into the thickest part of the pork.
10. Cover the hood and allow the grill to cook.
11. Mix scallions and other in a bowl.
12. Serve the pork with the scallions mixture.

PER SERVING

Calories 388 | Fat 8g | Sodium 611mg | Carbs 18g | Fiber 0g | Sugar 4g | Protein 13g

Steak Kabobs

Prep time: 10 minutes | Cooking time: 8 minutes | Serves 2

- 1-2 steaks
- 1 onion
- 1 bundle mushrooms
- 10-12 cherry tomatoes
- 1 bell pepper
- 2 - 2 ½ cup Italian Dressing
- Wooden or Metal Skewers

1. Cut steaks about 1-inch strips. Soak wooden skewers in water for at least 30 minutes. Or they will burn up.
2. Pour Italian dressing over the steak and let it marinate while prep vegetables.
3. Wash and prep vegetables. The mushrooms whole and tomatoes whole and sliced the pepper and onions in around 1-inch pieces.
4. Once skewers have been soaked in water, if using wood, start pushing steak and vegetables onto the skewers.
5. Place in a dish and then pour the dressing over the top of the veggies and meat. Then cover and let marinate for 3-4 hours in the fridge.
6. Preheat Ninja Foodi Grill. Select the GRILL setting and MAX heat. Let it preheat, it takes about 12 minutes.
7. Once the grill is hot, carefully place your steak kabobs onto the grill. And you should cook 4-5 at a time.
8. Close lid and select 8 minutes. Flip at the 4-minute mark.
9. Cook steaks until it reaches your desired doneness. At 8 minutes our medium-well to well done. If you want rarer, cook for a bit less.
10. Once your steak skewers are done, remove with tong, and then remove from skewers and serve.
11. Enjoy these easy and delicious Ninja Foodi Grill steak kabobs any day of the week, and rain or shine.

PER SERVING

Calories 416 | Carbohydrates 17g | Protein 12g | Fat 33g | Sodium 1191mg | Fiber 1g

Grilled Pork Belly Kebabs
Prep time: 10 minutes|Cooking time: 10 minutes|Serves 4

- 2 tbsp. gochujang
- 2 tbsp. honey
- 2 tsp. sake
- 2 tsp. soy sauce
- 1 tsp. vegetable oil
- 1 ¼ lb. boneless pork belly, cut into cubes
- 1 small zucchini, cut 1-inch-thick half-moons
- ½ pint cherry tomatoes
- 1 red bell pepper, seeded, and cut into 1-inch pieces

1. Mix oil, soy sauce, sake, honey and gochujang in a bowl and keep 2 tbsp. of this marinade aside.
2. Add pork to the bowl, mix well, cover and refrigerate for 1 hour.
3. Thread the pork, bell pepper, tomatoes and zucchini on the wooden skewers alternately.
4. Place the cooking pot in the Ninja Foodi Smart XL Grill then set a grill grate inside.
5. Select the "Grill" Mode, set the temperature to MED.
6. Press the START/STOP button to initiate preheating.
7. Once preheated, place the pork in the Ninja Foodi Smart XL Grill.
8. Cover the hood and allow the grill to cook for 10 minutes, flipping halfway through.
9. Pour the reserved marinade on top of the skewers and serve warm.

PER SERVING

Calories 361 | Fat 16g |Sodium 515mg | Carbs 13g | Fiber 0.1g | Sugar 18.2g | Protein 33.3g

Grilled Pork Tenderloin Marinated in Spicy Soy Sauce
Prep time: 20 minutes|Cooking time: 140 minutes|Serves 6

- ¼ cup reduced-sodium soy sauce
- 1 tablespoon finely grated fresh ginger
- 2 tbsp sugar
- 1 large garlic clove, minced
- 1 fresh red Thai chile, minced
- 1 tablespoon toasted sesame oil
- 1½ pounds pork tenderloin, trimmed of fat and cut into 1-inch-thick medallions

1. Select the "GRILL" function and adjust temperature to "MED" and preheat the Ninja Foodi Smart XL Grill for 8 minutes.
2. Whisk the soy sauce and sugar in a medium bowl until the sugar is dissolved.
3. Stir in ginger, garlic, chili, and oil.
4. Place the pork in a plastic bag.
5. Add the marinade and then seal the bag, squeezing out the air.
6. Turn the bag for coating the medallions.
7. Refrigerate for two hours, turning bag once to redistribute the marinade.
8. Insert Grill Grate in the unit and close the hood.
9. Remove the pork from the marinade.
10. Select the option START/STOP to begin cooking.
11. Cook pork until desire tenderness or until meat reaches to 160°F internal temperature.

PER SERVING

Calories 155.5 | Carbohydrates 24.8g | Protein 3g | Fat 5.4g | Sodium 193.7mg| Fiber 1 g

Garlic Butter Pork
Prep time: 70 minutes|Cooking time: 10 minutes|Serves 4

- 1 tbsp. coconut butter
- 1 tbsp. coconut oil
- 2 tsp. cloves garlic, grated
- 2 tsp. parsley
- Salt and pepper to taste
- 4 pork chops, sliced into strips

1. Combine all the ingredients, except the pork strips. Mix them well.
2. Marinate the pork in the mixture for 1 hour.
3. Put the pork on the Ninja Foodi Grill.
4. Close the lid. Choose Air Fryer.
5. Cook at 400°F for 10 minutes.
6. Serve and enjoy.

PER SERVING

Calories: 388| Total Fat: 23.3g| Saturated Fat: 10.4g| Cholesterol: 69mg| Sodium: 57mg| Total Carbohydrate: 0.5g| Dietary Fiber: 0.1g| Total Sugars: 0g| Protein: 18.1g| Potassium: 285mg

Korean Pork

Prep time: 5-10 minutes | Cooking time: 8 minutes | Serves 4

- 2 lb. pork, cut into 1/8-inch slices
- 5 minced garlic cloves
- 3 tbsp. minced green onion
- 1 yellow onion, sliced
- ½ cup soy sauce
- ½ cup brown sugar
- 3 tbsp. Korean red chili paste or regular chili paste
- 2 tbsp. sesame seeds
- 3 tsp. black pepper
- Red pepper flakes to taste

1. Take a zip-lock bag, add all the ingredients. Shake well and refrigerate for 6-8 hours to marinate.
2. Take the Ninja Foodi Grill, arrange it over your kitchen platform and open the top lid.
3. Arrange the grill grate and close the top lid.
4. Press "GRILL" and select the "MED" grill function. Adjust the timer to 8 minutes and then press "START/STOP." The Ninja Foodi will start preheating.
5. The Ninja Foodi is preheated and ready to cook when it starts beeping. After you hear a beep, open the top lid.
6. Arrange the sliced pork over the grill grate.
7. Close the top lid and cook for 4 minutes. Now, open the top lid, flip the pork.
8. Close the top lid and cook for 4 more minutes.
9. Serve it warm with chopped lettuce, optional.

PER SERVING

Calories: 621 | Fat: 31g | Saturated Fat: 12.5g | Trans Fat: 0g | Carbohydrates: 29g Fiber 3g | Sodium: 1428mg | Protein: 53g

BBQ Beef Short Ribs

Prep time: 5 minutes | Cooking time: 50 minutes | Serves 2

- 2 Beef Short Ribs
- ¼ c Red Wine
- ¾ c Beef Stock
- ¼ c Diced Onion
- ½ c BBQ sauce
- Seasoning
- Seasoning salt
- Garlic Powder
- Onion Powder
- 1 Tbsp Cornstarch

1. Season the beef ribs with the seasonings.
2. Add the onion, wine, and broth to the bottom of the Foodi cooking bowl.
3. Close the toggle switch to sealing.
4. Pressure cook on manual, high, for 40 minutes.
5. Do a natural release for 10 minutes, and then carefully release any remaining pressure until the pin drops and its safe open the lid.
6. Remove the ribs to a plate.
7. Generously brush the BBQ sauce over the entire surface of the ribs. Place the ribs back into the pot, on the top rack of the air crisping rack.
8. Air crisps the ribs for 10 minutes at 350 degrees F. Feel free to flip them halfway through.
9. Remove the ribs to rest and take out the rack.
10. Mix up the slurry and pour into the pan juices in the pot to thicken.
11. Spoon over the ribs and enjoy!

PER SERVING

Calories 906 | Carbohydrates 78g | Protein 50g | Fat 22g | Sodium 2667mg | Fiber 3g

Curried Pork Skewers

Prep time: 10 minutes | Cooking time: 23 minutes | Serves 4

- 1 (13 ½ -oz.) can unsweetened coconut milk
- 2 tbsp. fish sauce
- 2 tbsp. Thai thin soy sauce
- 1 tbsp. sugar
- 1 tsp. kosher salt
- ¾ tsp. white pepper
- ½ tsp. curry powder
- ½ tsp. ground turmeric
- ¾ cup sweetened condensed milk
- 1 (1/2 lb.) boneless pork shoulder, cut into 4x ½ " strips
- 4 oz. fatback, cut into ½ " pieces

1. Mix coconut milk, turmeric, curry powder, black pepper, salt, sugar, soy sauce and fish sauce in a pan.
2. Cook to a boil then reduce its heat and cook for 15 minutes on a simmer.
3. Allow this mixture to cool, then add black pepper, salt and pork.
4. Mix well, cover and refrigerate for 1 hour.
5. Place the cooking pot in the Ninja Foodi Smart XL Grill then set a grill grate inside.
6. Select the "Grill" Mode, set the temperature to MED.
7. Press the START/STOP button to initiate preheating.
8. Once preheated, place the pork in the Ninja Foodi Smart XL Grill.
9. Cover the hood and allow the grill to cook for 8 minutes, flipping halfway through.
10. Serve warm.

PER SERVING

Calories 429 | Fat 17g | Sodium 422mg | Carbs 15g | Fiber 0g | Sugar 1g | Protein 41g

Steak and Potatoes
Prep time: 15 minutes | Cooking time: 45 minutes | Serves 4

- 3-4 potatoes russet
- 3 steak
- ¼ cup avocado oil
- 2 tbsp steak seasoning
- 1 tbsp sea salt

1. Wash potatoes, dry, and poke with a fork all over them.
2. Rub avocado oil all over each one so they are well saturated. Sprinkle salt on outsides and put into air fryer basket.
3. Close lid and set to 400 degrees F, AIR CRISP function, cook for 35 minutes. Flip, then cook for an additional 10 minutes or until middle is fork tender when poked.
4. Remove potatoes and cover with foil to keep them warm. Remove Crisper Basket and replace with grill piece inside machine. Select the "GRILL" function and adjust temperature to "HI" and preheat.
5. Sprinkle both sides of steak with seasoning and press down so it sticks well.
6. When Ninja Foodi Grill is done preheating it will say lift adds food. Add steaks now.
7. Sirloins cooked 8 minutes, flipping halfway through; filet cooked for 6 minutes, flipping after 4 minutes.
8. Remove once you feel it is done to your liking. Allow to rest for at least 5 minutes to maintain juiciness before cutting.

PER SERVING
Calories 572 | Carbohydrates 21g | Protein 38g | Fat 38g | Sodium 1849mg | Fiber 4g

Balinese Pork Satay
Prep time: 15 minutes | Cooking time: 15 minutes | Serves 4

- Spice Paste:
- 1 (1-inch) knob fresh turmeric, peeled
- 2 stalks lemongrass, sliced
- 8 garlic cloves, sliced
- 2 small shallots, sliced
- 3 wholes dried Pasilla chilli with seeds removed, chopped
- 2 tbsp. palm sugar
- 2 tsp. whole coriander seed
- 1 tbsp. whole white peppercorns
- Kosher salt, to taste
- 2 lbs. boneless pork shoulder, cut into cubes
- Glaze
- 1 cup Kecap manis
- ¼ cup sugar
- One (2-inch) knob ginger, chopped
- 4 medium garlic cloves, chopped
- Dipping Sauce
- 10 oz. roasted peanuts
- ¼ cup vegetable or canola oil
- 1 oz. tamarind pulp
- 1 tbsp. Kecap manis or fish sauce
- Water, as necessary
- Sugar, to taste

1. Blend all the spice paste ingredients in a mini-food processor.
2. Mix pork with the ¾ of the spice paste in a bowl.
3. Cover and refrigerate the pork for 45 minutes. Thread the pork on the wooden skewers.
4. Place the cooking pot in the Ninja Foodi Smart XL Grill then set a grill grate inside.
5. Select the "Grill" Mode, set the temperature to MED.
6. Press the START/STOP button to initiate preheating.
7. Once preheated, place the pork in the Ninja Foodi Smart XL Grill.
8. Cover the hood and allow the grill to cook for 10 minutes, flipping halfway through.
9. Meanwhile, mix the glaze ingredients and ⅓ spice paste in a saucepan and cook for 5 minutes on a simmer. Pour this glaze over the skewers. Serve warm.

PER SERVING
Calories 425 | Fat 14g | Sodium 411mg | Carbs 24g |

Fiber 0.3g | Sugar 1g | Protein 28.3g

Pork with Salsa
Prep time: 15 minutes | Cooking time: 12 minutes | Serves 4

- ¼ cup lime juice
- 2 garlic cloves, minced
- 1 ½ teaspoon ground cumin
- 1 ½ teaspoons dried oregano
- ½ teaspoon black pepper
- 2 pounds pork tenderloin, ¾ inch slices
- Salsa
- 1 jalapeno pepper, seeded and chopped
- ⅓ cup red onion, chopped
- 2 tablespoons fresh mint, chopped
- 2 tablespoons lime juice
- 4 cups pears, peeled and chopped
- 1 tablespoon lime zest, grated
- 1 teaspoon sugar
- ½ teaspoon black pepper

1. Season the pork with lime juice, cumin, oregano, oil, garlic and pepper in a suitable bowl.
2. Cover to refrigerate for overnight margination.
3. Place the cooking pot in the Ninja Foodi Smart XL Grill then place the grill grate in the pot.
4. Select the "Grill" Mode, set the temperature to MAX.
5. Place the pork in the Ninja Foodi Smart XL Grill.
6. Cover the hood and allow the grill to cook for 6 minutes per side until al dente.
7. Mix the pear salsa into a separate bowl.
8. Serve the sliced pork with pear salsa.

PER SERVING
Calories 91 | Fat 5g | Sodium 88mg | Carbs 3g | Fiber 0g | Sugar 0g | Protein 7g

Chapter 5
Seafood Recipes

Grilled Ahi Tuna

Prep time: 10 minutes|Cooking time: 9 minutes|Serves 2

- 1 cup labneh yogurt
- ⅓ cup chives, chopped
- 2 garlic cloves, minced
- 2 tsp. lemon zest
- 1 tbsp. fresh lemon juice
- 1 ½ tsp. kosher salt
- 3 tbsp. olive oil
- ¼ tsp. black pepper
- 2 (6-oz.) ahi tuna steaks, 1 ½ "-thick
- 10 oz. broccolini, stems trimmed
- ¼ tsp. crushed red pepper

1. Mix labneh, chives, garlic, lemon zest and juice, and ½ tsp. salt in a small bowl.
2. Season the turn steaks wit 1 tbsp. oil, ¼ tsp. black pepper, and ½ tsp. salt.
3. Place the cooking pot in the Ninja Foodi Smart XL Grill then set a grill grate inside.
4. Plug the thermometer into the appliance.
5. Select the "Grill" Mode, set the temperature to MED then select the PRESET.
6. Use the right arrow keys on the display to select "FISH" and set the doneness to MED WELL.
7. Press the START/STOP button to initiate preheating.
8. Once preheated, place the tuna fillets in the Ninja Foodi Smart XL Grill.
9. Insert the thermometer probe into the thickest part of the fish.
10. Cover the hood and allow the grill to cook.
11. Toss broccolini with red pepper, ½ tsp. salt and 2 tbsp. olive oil in a bowl.
12. Grill them for 5 minutes in the Ninja Smart grill.
13. Serve the turn steaks with labneh, and broccolini.

PER SERVING

Calories 392 | Fat 16g |Sodium 466mg | Carbs 19g | Fiber 0.9g | Sugar 0.6g | Protein 48g

Grilled Coconut and Pineapple Sweet Chili Shrimp

Prep time: 15 minutes|Cooking time: 6 minutes|Serves 4

- Sweet chili sauce:
- 3 tbsp. coconut cream
- 3 tbsp. pineapple sweet chili sauce
- 1 tsp. sriracha
- Grilled shrimp
- 1 lb. shrimp, peeled and deveined
- 2 slices pineapple, cut into ½ inch pieces

1. Mix the chili sauce in a bowl.
2. Toss in shrimp and pineapple then mix well to coat.
3. Thread the shrimp and pineapple on the wooden skewers alternately.
4. Place the cooking pot in the Ninja Foodi Smart XL Grill then set a grill grate inside.
5. Select the "Grill" Mode, set the temperature to MED.
6. Press the START/STOP button to initiate preheating.
7. Once preheated, place the skewers in the Ninja Foodi Smart XL Grill.
8. Cover the hood and allow the grill to cook for 6 minutes, flipping halfway through.
9. Serve warm.

PER SERVING

Calories 309 | Fat 25g |Sodium 463mg | Carbs 9.9g | Fiber 0.3g | Sugar 0.3g | Protein 18g

Grilled Calamari

Prep time: 15 minutes|Cooking time: 22 minutes|Serves 4

- 1 garlic clove, chopped
- 2 ½ tbsp. olive oil
- 3 ¼ tsp. kosher salt
- 1 lb. (10 small) calamari
- 3 large red bell peppers, chopped
- 2 tsp. sherry vinegar
- 10 fresh mint leaves

1. Mix garlic with 1 ½ tbsp. oil, salt, and calamari in a bowl.
2. Cover and refrigerate them for 10 minutes.
3. Place the cooking pot in the Ninja Foodi Smart XL Grill then set a grill grate inside.
4. Plug the thermometer into the appliance.
5. Select the "Bake" Mode, set the temperature to 400 degrees F.
6. Set the cooking time to 20 minutes.
7. Press the START/STOP button to initiate preheating.
8. Once preheated, place the peppers in the Ninja Foodi Smart XL Grill.
9. Cover the hood and allow the grill to cook then flip once cooked halfway through.
10. Cut the peppers in half, remove the seeds and cut into strips.
11. Mix these peppers with 1 tbsp. oil, ¼ tsp. salt, and vinegar in a bowl.
12. Grill the calamari in the Ninja Foodi Smart XL Grill for 1 minute per side
13. Serve the calamari with peppers mixture and garnish with mint.
14. Enjoy.

PER SERVING

Calories 448 | Fat 13g |Sodium 353mg | Carbs 3g | Fiber 0.4g | Sugar 1g | Protein 29g

Tuna Burgers

Prep time: 10 minutes | Cooking time: 10 minutes | Serves 4

- 1¼ lb. fresh tuna
- 2 scallions, chopped
- 12 pitted kalamata olives
- 1 tbsp. salted capers
- Salt, to taste
- Black pepper, to taste
- Olive oil, to taste
- ¼ cup mayonnaise
- 1½ tsp. anchovy paste
- 4 brioche buns
- Sliced tomatoes
- Arugula, to serve

1. Blend tuna with scallions, olives and oil in a food processor for 1 minute.
2. Make 4- 4 inch round patties out of this mixture.
3. Place the cooking pot in the Ninja Foodi Smart XL Grill then set a grill grate inside.
4. Select the "Bake" Mode, set the temperature to 400 degrees F.
5. Press the START/STOP button to initiate preheating.
6. Once preheated, place the patties in the Ninja Foodi Smart XL Grill.
7. Cover the hood and allow the grill to cook for 10 minutes, flipping halfway through.
8. Top the bottom half of the buns with mayo, anchovy paste, burgers, tomatoes, and rest of the .
9. Once preheated, place the other half of the buns on top.
10. Serve.

PER SERVING

Calories 376 | Fat 17g | Sodium 1127mg | Carbs 24g | Fiber 1g | Sugar 3g | Protein 29g

Grilled Scallops

Prep time: 15 minutes | Cooking time: 6 minutes | Serves 6

- ⅓ cup mayonnaise
- 2 tsp. fresh lime juice
- Kosher salt, to taste
- 1 toasted nori sheet
- 1 tsp. ground coriander
- ½ tsp. ground ginger
- 2 tbsp. vegetable oil
- 12 large dry sea scallops
- ½ lime
- 3 scallions, sliced
- 1 tsp. Aleppo pepper flakes

1. Mix mayonnaise with 1 tbsp. water, 1 pinch of salt, and lime juice in a bowl.
2. Grind nori and mix half of it with ginger, coriander, and 2 tbsp. oil in a bowl
3. Stir in scallops, mix well to coat and thread them on the wooden skewers.
4. Place the cooking pot in the Ninja Foodi Smart XL Grill then set a grill grate inside.
5. Select the "Grill" Mode, set the temperature to MED.
6. Once preheated, place the scallops in the Ninja Foodi Smart XL Grill.
7. Cover the hood and allow the grill to cook for 6 minutes, flipping halfway through.
8. Spread lime mayo on a plate and top it with scallop skewers and garnish with nori, pepper, lime juice and scallions.
9. Serve warm.

PER SERVING

Calories 405 | Fat 22.7g | Sodium 227mg | Carbs 6.1g | Fiber 1.4g | Sugar 0.9g | Protein 45.2g

Scallops with Creamed Corn

Prep time: 10 minutes | Cooking time: 27 minutes | Serves 4

- 3 dried Pasilla chiles, chopped
- 2 tbsp. dried thyme
- 1 tbsp. dried oregano
- 1 tbsp. ground coriander
- 1 tbsp. ground fennel
- 2 tsp. chipotle chile powder
- 2 tsp. black pepper
- 2 tsp. paprika
- 1 tsp. garlic powder
- 1 tsp. onion powder
- Zest of 1 lime
- 1 lb. large sea scallops
- 2 tbsp. olive oil
- 4 green garlic, sliced
- 1 medium shallot, chopped
- 1 garlic clove, sliced
- 4 ears of corn, husked, kernels grated
- 1 tbsp. unsalted butter
- Kosher salt, to taste
- Vegetable oil, for drizzling
- Lime wedges, for serving

1. Grind Pasilla chiles in a spice milk and mix them with onion power, garlic powder, paprika, black pepper, chile powder, fennel, coriander, oregano and thyme in a bowl.
2. Mix scallops with 2 tbsp. rub and lime zest in a bowl.
3. Stir in grated corn and cook for 5 minutes.
4. Add water and cook for 18 minutes until it is absorbed.
5. Stir in salt and butter for seasoning.
6. Thread the scallops on the skewers and season them with salt and oil.
7. Select the "Grill" Mode, set the temperature to LOW.
8. Press the START/STOP button to initiate preheating.
9. Cover the Ninja Foodi Grill's hood and cook for 3 minutes per side.
10. Serve the scallops on top of the creamed corn.

PER SERVING

Calories 301 | Fat 5g | Sodium 340mg | Carbs 27g | Fiber 1.2g | Sugar 1.3g | Protein 15.3g

Shrimp Boil

Prep time: 10 minutes | Cooking time: 6 minutes | Serves 6

- 1 ½ lb. large shrimp, peeled and deveined
- 2 garlic cloves, minced
- 2 smoked andouille sausages, sliced
- 2 ears corn, cut into 4 pieces
- 1 lb. red bliss potatoes, chopped
- 2 tbsp. olive oil
- 3 tsp. Old Bay seasoning
- 1 lemon, sliced into thin wedges
- 4 tbsp. butter, melted
- Kosher salt, to taste
- Black pepper, to taste
- 2 tbsp. fresh parsley leaves, chopped

1. Boil potatoes with water and a pinch of salt in a saucepan and cook until soft.
2. Mix shrimp with 1 tbsp. parsley, 2 tsp. old bay, garlic, and oil in a bowl.
3. Toss potatoes with 1 tbsp. parsley, 1 tsp. old bay, melted and melted butter then mix well.
4. Thread the shrimp, potatoes, corn and sausage on the wooden skewers.
5. Set a grill grate in the Ninja Foody Smart XL pot.
6. Select the "Grill" Mode, set the temperature to HI.
7. Press the START/STOP button to initiate preheating.
8. Once preheated, place the shrimp skewers in the Ninja Foodi Smart XL Grill.
9. Cook for 6 minutes. Flip the skewers once cooked halfway through.
10. Serve warm.

PER SERVING

Calories 457 | Fat 19g | Sodium 557mg | Carbs 29g | Fiber 1.8g | Sugar 1.2g | Protein 32.5g

Pineapple Shrimp Skewers

Prep time: 10 minutes | Cooking time: 6 minutes | Serves 6-8

- 3 cups pineapple, cubed
- 1 lb. shrimp, peeled and deveined
- 3 tbsp. olive oil
- 3 tbsp. sweet chili sauce
- 2 garlic cloves, minced
- 2 tsp. freshly grated ginger
- 2 tsp. toasted sesame oil crushed red pepper flakes
- ½ tsp. crushed red pepper flakes
- Kosher salt
- Toasted sesame seeds, for garnish
- Thinly sliced green onions, for garnish
- Lime wedges, for serving

1. Toss shrimp with the in a bowl.
2. Thread the shrimp and pineapple on the skewers.
3. Place the cooking pot in the Ninja Foodi Smart XL Grill then set a grill grate inside.
4. Select the "Grill" Mode, set the temperature to MED.
5. Press the START/STOP button to initiate preheating.
6. Once preheated, place the skewers in the Ninja Foodi Smart XL Grill.
7. Cover the hood and allow the grill to cook for 6 minutes, flipping halfway through.
8. Serve warm.

PER SERVING

Calories 321 | Fat 7.4g | Sodium 356mg | Carbs 19g | Fiber 2.4g | Sugar 5g | Protein 37.2g

Grilled Oysters

Prep time: 10 minutes | Cooking time: 7 minutes | Serves 4

- 2 cups butter, softened
- ½ cup Parmesan cheese, grated
- ¼ cup parsley, chopped
- 2 garlic cloves, minced
- 1 tbsp. Worcestershire sauce
- 1 tsp. paprika
- ½ tsp. ground red pepper
- ½ tsp. hot sauce
- 2 dozen large fresh oysters on the half shell

1. Blend butter with parmesan cheese, parsley, garlic, paprika, red pepper, and hot sauce in a food processor.
2. Stuff the oysters with this mixture.
3. Place the cooking pot in the Ninja Foodi Smart XL Grill then set a grill grate inside.
4. Select the "Grill" Mode, set the temperature to MED.
5. Use the arrow keys on the display to select the cooking time to 5 minutes.
6. Press the START/STOP button to initiate preheating.
7. Once preheated, place the oysters in the Ninja Foodi Smart XL Grill.
8. Cover the hood and allow the grill to cook.
9. Serve warm.

PER SERVING

Calories 395 | Fat 9.5g | Sodium 655mg | Carbs 3.4g | Fiber 0.4g | Sugar 0.4g | Protein 28.3g

Grilled Shrimp Tostadas with Guacamole

Prep time: 10 minutes | Cooking time: 14 minutes | Serves 8

- 8 (6") corn tortillas
- Cooking spray
- 3 ripe avocados, diced
- 1 small shallot, minced
- 7 tbsp. lime juice
- 3 tbsp. freshly chopped cilantro
- Kosher salt, to taste
- 2 tsp. cumin
- ½ tsp. cayenne
- ¼ cup olive oil
- 24 medium shrimp, peeled and deveined
- Black pepper, to taste
- ¼ cup red cabbage, shredded
- ¾ cup carrots, shredded
- Cilantro leaves, for serving
- Lime wedges, for serving

1. Place the cooking pot in the Ninja Foodi Smart XL Grill then set a grill grate inside.
2. Select the "Grill" Mode, set the temperature to MED.
3. Press the START/STOP button to initiate preheating.
4. Use the arrow keys to set the cooking time to 4 minutes.
5. Once preheated, grill the tortillas in the Ninja Foodi Smart XL Grill then transfer to a plate.
6. Mash avocados with salt, cilantro, 3 tbsp. lime juice, and shallot in a bowl.
7. Mix shrimp with oil, black pepper, salt, 2 tbsp. oil, 2 tbsp. lime juice, cayenne and cumin in a bowl.
8. Place the shrimp in the Ninja Foodi Smart XL Grill.
9. Cover the Ninja Foodi Smart XL Grill's hood, select the Bake Mode, set the temperature to 350 degrees F and cook for 3 minutes.
10. Flip the shrimp and cook again for 3 minutes.
11. Toss carrots and cabbage with 2 tbsp. lime juice, black pepper, salt and 2 tbsp. oil.
12. Divide the cabbage mixture, guacamole and shrimp in the tortillas.
13. Serve warm.

PER SERVING

Calories 345 | Fat 36g | Sodium 272mg | Carbs 21g | Fiber 0.2g | Sugar 0.1g | Protein 22.5g

Shrimp and Chorizo Grill

Prep time: 10 minutes | Cooking time: 46 minutes | Serves 4

- Cilantro-Sour Cream Sauce
- 1¼ cups sour cream
- 1 cup cilantro leaves with tender stems
- ¼ cup mayonnaise
- 1 small jalapeño, sliced
- 2 tbsp. fresh lime juice
- 1¼ tsp. kosher salt
- Dressing
- 5 tbsp. olive oil
- ¼ cup fresh lime juice
- 1 garlic clove, grated
- 2 tbsp. cilantro, chopped
- 1 tsp. honey
- 1 tsp. kosher salt
- Grilling and Assembly
- 1½ lb. jumbo or large shrimp, peeled, deveined
- ½ tsp. chili powder
- 1¼ tsp. kosher salt
- 1 head of green cabbage, cut into 4 wedges
- 6 links fresh chorizo sausage (1½ lb.)
- Canola oil (for grill)
- 2 bunches medium or large asparagus, tough ends trimmed
- Lime wedges (for serving)

1. Blend all the ingredients for sour cream sauce in a blender.
2. Mix lime juice and rest of the dressing ingredients in a bowl.
3. Season the shrimp with 1 tsp. salt, and chili powder in a bowl.
4. Place the cooking pot in the Ninja Foodi Smart XL Grill then set a grill grate inside.
5. Select the "Grill" Mode, set the temperature to MED.
6. Press the START/STOP button to initiate preheating.
7. Once preheated, place the shrimp in the Ninja Foodi Smart XL Grill.
8. Cover the hood and allow the grill to cook for 20 minutes with flipping halfway through, then transfer to a plate.
9. Grill the sausages for 7 minutes per side and transfer to the plate.
10. Now grill the asparagus in the Ninja Foodi Smart Grill for 3 minutes per side then transfer them to plate.
11. Finally grill the shrimp for 3 minutes per side and add them to the veggies.
12. Garnish with the lime wedges.
13. Serve.

PER SERVING

Calories 337 | Fat 20g | Sodium 719mg | Carbs 11g | Fiber 0.9g | Sugar 1.4g | Protein 37.8g

Nigerian Skewers

Prep time: 10 minutes| Cooking time: 41 minutes|Serves 6

- Spice blend
- 3 tbsp. cayenne pepper
- 1½ tbsp. roasted peanuts
- 1 tbsp. paprika
- 1 tbsp. garlic powder
- 1 tbsp. onion powder
- ½ tbsp. ground ginger
- 2 tsp. kosher salt
- 2 Maggi bouillon cubes, crushed
- Suya:
- 1 lb. jumbo shrimp, peeled and deveined
- 1 lb. Wagyu rib eye beef, thinly sliced
- 1 lb. boneless chicken thighs, cut into 2-inch pieces
- For the roasted tomato soubise:
- 2 medium vine-ripened tomatoes, stemmed
- 1 tbsp. olive oil
- Kosher salt, to taste
- 2 tbsp. canola oil
- 1 medium white onion, sliced
- 1 cup heavy cream

1. Blend cayenne pepper and other ingredients in a bowl.
2. Divide this marinade in three bowls and add chicken, beef and shrimp to the bowls.
3. Mix well to coat, cover and refrigerate them for 1 hour.
4. Toss tomatoes with salt and olive oil in a bowl.
5. Place the cooking pot in the Ninja Foodi Smart XL Grill then set a grill grate inside.
6. Select the "Grill" Mode, set the temperature to MED.
7. Use the arrow keys to set the time to 14 minutes.
8. Press the START/STOP button to initiate preheating.
9. Once preheated, place the tomatoes in the Ninja Foodi Smart XL Grill.
10. Cover the hood and allow the grill to cook then transfer to a plate.
11. Sauté onion with oil in a skillet for 6 minutes.
12. Stir in baked tomatoes and sauté for 10 minutes.
13. Add cream and blend this mixture with salt in a blender.
14. Thread the marinated chicken, beef and shrimp on the separated skewers.
15. Once preheated, place the skewers in the Ninja Foodi Smart XL Grill.
16. Grill the beef skewers for 3 minutes per side, chicken for 4 minutes per side and shrimp 2 minutes per side.
17. Serve warm with the tomato soubise.

PER SERVING

Calories 248 | Fat 23g |Sodium 350mg | Carbs 18g | Fiber 6.3g | Sugar 1g | Protein 40.3g

Shrimp with Tomatoes

Prep time: 15 minutes| Cooking time: 8 minutes|Serves 6

- ⅔ cup fresh arugula
- ⅓ cup lemon juice
- 2 tablespoons olive oil
- 2 garlic cloves, minced
- ½ teaspoon grated lemon zest
- 1 pound uncooked shrimp, peeled and deveined
- 2 green onions, sliced
- ¼ cup plain yogurt
- 2 teaspoons 2% milk
- 1 teaspoon cider
- 1 teaspoon Dijon mustard
- ½ teaspoon sugar
- ½ teaspoon salt
- 12 cherry tomatoes
- ¼ teaspoon black pepper

1. Season the shrimp with lemon juice, lemon zest, oil and garlic in a suitable bowl.
2. Let it set for 10 minutes of margination.
3. Now arugula, yogurt, milk, green onion, sugar, vinegar, mustard and ¼ teaspoon salt in a blender.
4. Thread the seasoned shrimp and tomatoes on the skewers alternately.
5. Season the skewers with salt and black pepper.
6. Place the cooking pot in the Ninja Foodi Smart XL Grill then place the grill grate in the pot.
7. Select the "Grill" Mode, set the temperature to MED.
8. Press the START/STOP button to initiate preheating.
9. Once preheated, place the skewers in the Ninja Foodi Smart XL Grill.
10. Cover the hood and allow the grill to cook for 2 minutes per side.
11. Cook the shrimp in batches.
12. Serve with the prepared sauce.

PER SERVING

Calories 448 | Fat 13g | Sodium 353mg | Carbs 31g | Fiber 0.4g | Sugar 1g | Protein 29g

Chapter 6
Vegetarian Recipes

Charred Asparagus Tacos

Prep time: 15 minutes | Cooking time: 22 minutes | Serves 24

- 2 ancho chilies, stemmed and seeded
- 2 tbsp. vegetable oil
- 1 small onion, sliced
- 2 garlic cloves, grated on
- 2 tsp. dried oregano
- 1 tbsp. cider vinegar
- 1 chipotle chili
- 1 tbsp. sauce from chipotles
- ⅔ cup sour cream or Mexican crema
- 2 tsp. fresh juice from 2 limes
- Kosher salt and black pepper, to taste
- 2 ½ lbs. asparagus, cut into 1-inch segments
- 24 corn tortillas warmed
- Pickled red onion, to serve
- Queso fresco or queso cotija, to serve
- Fresh cilantro leaves, to serve
- Lime wedges, to serve

1. Sauté ancho chilies in a saucepan for 3 minutes then soak in water for 3 minutes then drain and reserve the liquid.
2. Sauté onion with 1 tbsp. oil in a skillet for 8 minutes.
3. Stir in oregano and garlic then sauté for 30 seconds.
4. Add chili liquid, chili sauce, chipotle chile and vinegar, mix well then blend with lime juice, sour cream and soaked chilies in a blender.
5. Stir in black pepper and salt for seasoning.
6. Toss asparagus with oil, black pepper and salt in a bowl.
7. Place the cooking pot in the Ninja Foodi Smart XL Grill.
8. Select the Bake Mode and set the temperature to 350 degrees F.
9. Use the Arrow keys to set the time to 10 minutes.
10. Press the Start/Stop button to initiate preheating.
11. Once preheated, place the asparagus in the Ninja Foodi Smart XL Grill.
12. Cover the hood and allow the grill to cook.
13. Divide the prepared sauce in the tortillas and add asparagus on top.
14. Garnish with lime wedges, cilantro, cheese and onions
15. Serve warm.

PER SERVING

Calories 93 | Fat 3g | Sodium 510mg | Carbs 22g | Fiber 3g | Sugar 4g | Protein 4g

Eggplant Caprese

Prep time: 15 minute | Cooing time: 10 minutes | Serves 2

- 1 large eggplant, cut into ¼ -inch slices
- 1 ball fresh mozzarella, cut into ¼ -inch slices
- 2 large tomatoes, cut into ¼ -inch slices
- ¼ cup of basil chiffonade
- 1 tbsp. Kosher salt
- Olive oil, as required
- Balsamic vinegar, as required
- Black pepper, to taste

1. Keep eggplant slices in a colander and sprinkle salt on top then leave for leave for 30 minutes.
2. Place the cooking pot in the Ninja Foodi Smart XL Grill.
3. Select the Bake Mode and set the temperature to 350 degrees F.
4. Use the Arrow keys to set the time to 10 minutes.
5. Press the Start/Stop button to initiate preheating.
6. Once preheated, place the eggplants in the Ninja Foodi Smart XL Grill.
7. Cover the hood and allow the grill to cook.
8. Place one tomato slice and cheese slice on top of the eggplant slices.
9. Garnish with- basil and serve.

PER SERVING

Calories 351 | Fat 19g | Sodium 412mg | Carbs 13g | Fiber 0.3g | Sugar 1g | Protein 3g

Cool Rosemary Potatoes

Prep time: 10 minutes | Cooking time: 20 minutes | Serves 4

- 2 pounds baby red potatoes, quartered
- ½ tsp parsley, dried
- ¼ tsp celery powder
- 2 tbsp extra virgin olive oil
- ¼ cup onion flakes, dried
- ½ tsp garlic powder
- ½ tsp onion powder
- ½ tsp salt
- ¼ tsp freshly ground black pepper

1. Add all listed ingredients into a large bowl.
2. Toss well and coat them well.
3. Pre-heat your Ninja Foodi by pressing the "AIR CRISP" option and setting it to 390 Degrees F.
4. Set the timer to 20 minutes.
5. Allow it to pre-heat until it beeps.
6. Once preheated, add potatoes to the cooking basket.
7. Close the lid and cook for 10 minutes.
8. Shake the basket and cook for 10 minutes more.
9. Check the crispness if it is done or not.
10. Cook for 5 minutes more if needed.
11. Serve and enjoy!

PER SERVING

Calories: 232 | Fat: 7 g | Carbohydrates: 39 g | Fiber: 6 g | Sodium: 249 mg | Protein: 4 g

Tomato Salsa
Prep time: 5-10 minutes|Cooking time: 10 minutes|Serves 4

- 1 red onion, peeled, cut in quarters
- 1 jalapeño pepper, cut in half, seeds removed
- 5 Roma tomatoes, cut in half lengthwise
- 1 tablespoon kosher salt
- 2 tsp ground black pepper
- 2 tbsp canola oil
- 1 bunch cilantro, stems trimmed
- Juice and zest of 3 limes
- 3 cloves garlic, peeled
- 2 tbsp ground cumin

1. In a blending bowl, join the onion, tomatoes, jalapeño pepper, salt, dark pepper, and canola oil.
2. Take Ninja Foodi Grill, mastermind it over your kitchen stage, and open the top. Mastermind the barbecue mesh and close the top cover.
3. Press "GRILL" and select the "MAX" flame broil work. Change the clock to 10 minutes and afterward press "START/STOP." Ninja Foodi will begin preheating.
4. Ninja Foodi is preheated and prepared to cook when it begins to blare. After you hear a signal, open the top cover.
5. Arrange the vegetables over the Grill Grate.
6. Close the top lid and cook for 5 minutes. Now open the top lid, flip the vegetables.
7. Close the top lid and cook for 5 more minutes.
8. Blend the mixture in a blender and serve as needed.

PER SERVING
Calories: 169| Fat: 9g|Carbohydrates: 12g| Fiber: 3g| Sodium: 321mg| Protein: 2.5g

Potatoes in a Foil
Prep time: 15 minutes|Cooking time: 25 minutes|Serves 4

- 2 ½ pounds potatoes, peeled and diced
- 1 medium onion, chopped
- 5 bacon strips, cooked and crumbled
- ¼ cup butter, melted
- ½ teaspoon salt
- ¼ teaspoon black pepper
- 6 slices American cheese
- Sour cream, to serve

1. Toss potatoes with salt, pepper, butter, bacon and onion.
2. Add this mixture to a suitably sized foil sheet and wrap it well to seal.
3. Place the potato pockets in the Ninja Foodi Smart XL Grill.
4. Cover the Ninja Foodi Smart XL Grill's Hood, set the temperature to 350 degrees F and cook on the Bake mode for 15-25 minutes.
5. Drizzle cheese over hot potatoes.
6. Serve warm.

PER SERVING
Calories 378 | Fat 3.8g | Sodium 620mg | Carbs 13.3g | Fiber 2.4g | Sugar 1.2g | Protein 5.4g

Veggie Kabobs
Prep time: 10 minutes|Cooking time: 12 minutes|Serves 4

- 2 medium zucchinis, cut into 1" thick half-moons
- 1 (10-oz.) package baby bella mushrooms, cleaned and halved
- 1 medium red onion, cut into wedges
- 2 small lemons, cut into eighths
- 3 tbsp. olive oil
- 1 garlic clove, grated
- 1 tsp. thyme, chopped
- Pinch of crushed red pepper flakes
- Kosher salt, to taste
- Black pepper, to taste

1. Toss all the veggies with other ingredients in a bowl.
2. Place the cooking pot in the Ninja Foodi Smart XL Grill.
3. Select the Bake Mode and set the temperature to 350 degrees F.
4. Use the Arrow keys to set the time to 6 minutes.
5. Press the Start/Stop button to initiate preheating.
6. Once preheated, place the skewers in the Ninja Foodi Smart XL Grill.
7. Cover the hood and allow the grill to cook.
8. Flip the skewers and cook again for 6 minutes.
9. Serve warm.

PER SERVING
Calories 304 | Fat 31g |Sodium 834mg | Carbs 14g | Fiber 0.2g | Sugar 0.3g | Protein 4.6g

Delicious Broccoli and Arugula
Prep time: 10 minutes|Cooking time: 12 minutes|Serves 4

- Pepper as needed
- ½ tsp salt
- Red pepper flakes
- 2 tbsp extra virgin olive oil
- 1 tablespoon canola oil
- ½ red onion, sliced
- 1 garlic clove, minced
- 1 tsp Dijon mustard
- 1 tsp honey
- 1 tablespoon lemon juice
- 2 tbsp parmesan cheese, grated
- 4 cups arugula, torn
- 2 heads broccoli, trimmed

1. Pre-heat your Ninja Foodi Grill on GRILL mode at MAX heat and set the timer to 12 minutes.
2. Take a large-sized bowl and add broccoli, sliced onion, and canola oil, toss the mixture well until coated.
3. Once you hear the beep, it is pre-heated.
4. Arrange your vegetables over the grill grate; let them grill for 8-12 minutes.
5. Take a medium-sized bowl and whisk in lemon juice, olive oil, mustard, honey, garlic, red pepper flakes, pepper, and salt.
6. Once done, add the prepared veggies and arugula in a bowl.
7. Drizzle the prepared vinaigrette on top, sprinkle a bit of parmesan.
8. Stir and mix.
9. Enjoy!

PER SERVING
Calories: 168| Fat: 12 g| Carbohydrates: 13 g| Fiber: 1 g| Sodium: 392 mg| Protein: 6 g

Chinese Eggplant
Prep time: 10 minutes|Cooking time: 20 minutes|Serves 6

- 3 tbsp. sugar
- 3 tbsp. sake
- 2 tbsp. mirin
- 1 tbsp. rice vinegar
- ⅓ cup Shiro miso
- 1 tbsp. fresh ginger, grated
- ¼ cup vegetable oil
- 1 tsp. dark sesame oil
- 6 Chinese eggplants, halved lengthwise
- Toasted sesame seeds for garnish

1. Toss eggplants with rest of the ingredients in a bowl.
2. Place the cooking pot in the Ninja Foodi Smart XL Grill.
3. Select the Bake Mode and set the temperature to 350 degrees F.
4. Use the Arrow keys to set the time to 20 minutes.
5. Press the Start/Stop button to initiate preheating.
6. Once preheated, place the eggplants in the Ninja Foodi Smart XL Grill.
7. Cover the hood and allow the grill to cook.
8. Serve warm with the rest of the marinade on top.

PER SERVING
Calories 378 | Fat 3.8g |Sodium 620mg | Carbs 33g | Fiber 2.4g | Sugar 1.2g | Protein 5.4g

Mustard Green Veggie Meal
Prep time: 10 minutes|Cooking time: 30-40 minutes|Serves 4

- Vinaigrette
- 2 tbsp Dijon mustard
- 1 tsp salt
- ¼ tsp black pepper
- ½ cup avocado oil
- ½ olive oil
- ½ cup red wine vinegar
- 2 tbsp honey
- Veggies
- 4 sweet onions, quartered
- 4 yellow squash, cut in half
- 4 red peppers, seeded and halved
- 4 zucchinis, halved
- 2 bunches green onions, trimmed

1. Take a small bowl and whisk mustard, pepper, honey, vinegar, and salt.
2. Add oil to make a smooth mixture.
3. Mastermind the flame broil mesh and close the top cover.
4. Pre-heat Ninja Foodi by pressing the "GRILL" option and setting it to "MEDIUM".
5. Let it pre-heat until you hear a beep.
6. Arrange the onion quarters over the grill grate, lock lid and cook for 5 minutes.
7. Flip the peppers and cook for 5 minutes more.
8. Grill the other vegetables in the same manner with 7 minutes each side for zucchini, pepper, and squash and 1 minute for onion.
9. Prepare the vinaigrette by mixing all the ingredients under vinaigrette in a bowl.

PER SERVING
Calories: 326| Fat: 4.5 g| Carbohydrates: 35 g| Fiber: 4 g| Sodium: 543 mg| Protein: 8 g

Vegetable Orzo Salad

Prep time: 15 minutes | Cooking time: 14 minutes | Serves 4

- 1-¼ cups orzo, uncooked
- ½-lb. fresh asparagus, trimmed
- 1 zucchini, sliced
- 1 sweet yellow, halved
- 1 portobello mushroom, stem removed
- ½ red onion, halved
- Salad
- ½ teaspoon salt
- 1 cup grape tomatoes, halved
- 1 tablespoon minced fresh parsley
- 1 tablespoon minced fresh basil
- ¼ teaspoon black pepper
- 1 cup (4 oz.) feta cheese, crumbled
- Dressing
- 4 garlic cloves, minced
- ⅓ cup olive oil
- ¼ cup balsamic vinegar
- 3 tablespoons lemon juice
- 1 teaspoon lemon-pepper seasoning

1. Cook the orzo as per the given instructions on the package, then drain.
2. Toss all the salad and dressing in a bowl until well coated.
3. Preheat the Ninja Foodi Grill on the "Grill Mode" at MEDIUM-temperature settings.
4. Place the mushrooms, pepper, and onion in the Ninja Foodi grill.
5. Cover the grill's hood and grill for 5 minutes per side.
6. Now grill zucchini and asparagus for 2 minutes per side.
7. Dice the grilled veggies and add them to the salad bowl.
8. Mix well, then stir in orzo.
9. Give it a toss, then serve.

PER SERVING

Calories 246 | Fat 15g | Sodium 220mg | Carbs 40.3g | Fiber 2.4g | Sugar 1.2g | Protein 12.4g

Southwestern Potato Salad

Prep time: 15 minutes | Cooking time: 14 minutes | Serves 6

- 1-½ pound large red potatoes quartered lengthwise
- 3 tablespoons olive oil
- 2 Poblano peppers
- 2 medium ears sweet corn, husks removed
- ½ cup buttermilk
- ½ cup sour cream
- 1 tablespoon lime juice
- 1 Jalapeno pepper, seeded and minced
- 1 tablespoon minced fresh cilantro
- 1-½ teaspoons garlic salt
- 1 teaspoon ground cumin
- ¼ teaspoon Cayenne pepper

1. Add water and potatoes to a large saucepan and cook for five minutes on a boil.
2. Drain and rub the potatoes with oil.
3. Place the Poblanos in the Ninja Foodi Smart XL Grill.
4. Cover the Ninja Foodi Smart XL Grill's Hood, select the Grill mode, set the temperature to MED and cook for 5 minutes per side.
5. Now grill potatoes and corn for 7 minutes per side.
6. Peel the pepper and chop them.
7. Cut corn and potatoes as well and mix the peppers well in a bowl.
8. Whisk the rest of the ingredients in a separate bowl, then add to the potatoes.
9. Mix well and serve.

PER SERVING

Calories 338 | Fat 24g | Sodium 620mg | Carbs 58.3g | Fiber 2.4g | Sugar 1.2g | Protein 5.4g

Cheddar Cauliflower Meal

Prep time: 5-10 minutes | Cooking time: 15 minutes | Serves 2

- ½ tsp garlic powder
- ½ tsp paprika
- Ocean salt and ground dark pepper to taste
- 1 head cauliflower, stemmed and leaves removed
- 1 cup Cheddar cheese, shredded
- Ranch dressing, for garnish
- ¼ cup canola oil or vegetable oil
- 2 tbsp chopped chives
- 4 slices bacon, cooked and crumbled

1. Cut the cauliflower into 2-inch pieces.
2. In a blending bowl, include the oil, garlic powder, and paprika. Season with salt and ground dark pepper; join well. Coat the florets with the blend.
3. Take Ninja Foodi Grill, mastermind it over your kitchen stage, and open the top cover.
4. Mastermind the flame broil mesh and close the top cover.
5. Press "GRILL" and select the "MAX" heat. Change the clock to 15 minutes and afterward press "START/STOP." Ninja Foodi will begin preheating.
6. Ninja Foodi is preheated and prepared to cook when it begins to signal. After you hear a blare, open the top.
7. Organize the pieces over the Grill Grate.
8. Close the top lid and cook for 10 minutes. Now open the top lid, flip the pieces and top with the cheese.
9. Close the top lid and cook for 5 more minutes.

PER SERVING

Calories: 534 | Fat: 34g | Carbohydrates: 14.5g | Fiber: 4g | Sodium: 1359mg | Protein: 31g

Mushroom Tomato Roast

Prep time: 10 minutes | Cooking time: 15 minutes | Serves 4

- 2 cups cherry tomatoes
- 2 cups cremini button mushrooms
- ¼ cup of vinegar or ¼ cup of red wine
- 2 garlic cloves, finely chopped
- ½ cup extra-virgin olive oil
- 3 tbsp chopped thyme
- Pinch of crushed red pepper flakes
- 1 tsp kosher salt
- ½ tsp black pepper
- 6 scallions, cut crosswise into 2-inch pieces

1. Take a zip-lock bag; add black pepper, salt, red pepper flakes, thyme, vinegar, oil, and garlic. Add mushrooms, tomatoes, and scallions.
2. Shake well and refrigerate for 30-40 minutes to marinate.
3. Take Ninja Foodi Grill, orchestrate it over your kitchen stage, and open the top.
4. Press "ROAST" and alter the temperature to 400°F. Modify the clock to 12 minutes and afterward press "START/STOP." Ninja Foodi will begin preheating.
5. Ninja Foodi is preheated and prepared to cook when it begins to blare. After you hear a blare, open the top.
6. Arrange the mushroom mixture directly inside the pot.
7. Close the top lid and allow it to cook until the timer reads zero.
8. Arrange the mushroom mixture directly inside the Cooking Pot.

PER SERVING

Calories: 253 | Fat: 24g | Carbohydrates: 7g | Fiber: 2g | Sodium: 546mg | Protein: 1g

Grilled Brussels Sprouts with Bacon

Prep time: 10 minutes | Cooking time: 30 minutes | Serves 4

- ⅓ lb. thick cut bacon, diced
- 1 ½ lbs. Brussels sprouts
- 2 medium shallots, sliced
- Kosher salt, to taste
- Black pepper, to taste

1. Add 1 pinch salt and water to a pan and cook brussels sprouts for 5 minutes then drain.
2. Sauté bacon in a skillet for 5-10 minutes until crispy then transfer to a plate.
3. Add shallots to the bacon grease and sauté until brown then transfer to the bacon.
4. Toss brussels sprouts with bacon fat, black pepper and salt in a bowl.
5. Place the cooking pot in the Ninja Foodi Smart XL Grill then set a grill grate inside.
6. Select the "Grill" Mode, set the temperature to MED.
7. Use the arrow keys to set the cooking time to 10 minutes.
8. Press the START/STOP button to initiate preheating.
9. Once preheated, place the brussel sprouts in the Ninja Foodi Smart XL Grill.
10. Cover the hood and allow the grill to cook.
11. Flip the sprouts once cooked halfway through.
12. Add the baked Brussel sprouts to the bacon and toss well
13. Serve.

PER SERVING

Calories 341 | Fat 24g | Sodium 547mg | Carbs 14g | Fiber 1.2g | Sugar 1g | Protein 10.3g

Grilled Smashed Potatoes

Prep time: 15 minutes | Cooking time: 10 minutes | Serves 8

- 16 small potatoes, skinned
- 2 tbsp. olive oil
- 2 tbsp. fresh rosemary leaves, chopped
- Kosher salt, to taste
- Black pepper, to taste

1. Add potatoes, water and a pinch of salt to a saucepan, cook on a simmer for 20 minutes then drain.
2. Lightly smash the potatoes with your palm without breaking them.
3. Brush them with black pepper, salt and oil.
4. Place the cooking pot in the Ninja Foodi Smart XL Grill then set a grill grate inside.
5. Select the "Grill" Mode, set the temperature to MED.
6. Use the arrow keys to set the cooking time to 10 minutes.
7. Press the START/STOP button to initiate preheating.
8. Once preheated, place the potatoes in the Ninja Foodi Smart XL Grill.
9. Cover the hood and allow the grill to cook.
10. Flip the potatoes once cooked halfway through.
11. Serve warm.

PER SERVING

Calories 136 | Fat 20g | Sodium 249mg | Carbs 44g | Fiber 2g | Sugar 3g | Protein 4g

Buttery Spinach Meal

Prep time: 10 minutes | Cooking time: 15 minutes | Serves 4

- ⅔ cup olives, halved and pitted
- 1 and ½ cups feta cheese, grated
- 4 tbsp butter
- 2 pounds spinach, chopped and boiled
- Pepper and salt to taste
- 4 tsp lemon zest, grated

1. Take a mixing bowl and add spinach, butter, salt, pepper and mix well.
2. Pre-heat Ninja Foodi by pressing the "AIR CRISP" option and setting it to "340 Degrees F" and timer to 15 minutes.
3. Let it pre-heat until you hear a beep.
4. Arrange a reversible trivet in the Grill Pan, arrange spinach mixture in a basket and place basket in the trivet.
5. Let them cook until the timer runs out.
6. Serve and enjoy!

PER SERVING

Calories: 250 | Fat: 18 g | Carbohydrates: 8 g | Fiber: 3 g | Sodium: 309 mg | Protein: 10 g

Zucchini Rolls with Goat Cheese

Prep time: 15 minute | Cooking time: 12 minutes | Serves 4

- 1 small bunch fresh chives
- 4 medium zucchinis, cut into ¼" slices
- 3 tbsp. olive oil
- Kosher salt, to taste
- Black pepper, to taste
- 4 oz. fresh goat cheese
- 1 small fresh mint leaves, chopped
- 2 tbsp. balsamic vinegar
- 1 handful baby arugula
- 2 Fresno peppers, cut into 1/8" matchsticks

1. Blanch chives in a saucepan filled with water for 30 seconds then drain.
2. Brush the zucchini slices with black pepper, salt and oil.
3. Place the cooking pot in the Ninja Foodi Smart XL Grill then set a grill grate inside.
4. Select the "Grill" Mode, set the temperature to MED.
5. Use the arrow keys to set the cooking time to 6 minutes.
6. Press the START/STOP button to initiate preheating.
7. Once preheated, place the zucchini in the Ninja Foodi Smart XL Grill.
8. Cover the hood and allow the grill to cook.
9. Flip the zucchini once cooked halfway through.
10. Divide the goat cheese mint, balsamic vinegar, arugula and pepper on top of the grilled zucchini.
11. Roll the zucchini slices and seal with a toothpick.
12. Serve.

PER SERVING

Calories 224 | Fat 5g | Sodium 432mg | Carbs 3.1g | Fiber 0.3g | Sugar 1g | Protein 5.7g

Zucchini with Parmesan

Prep time: 15 minutes | Cooking time: 12 minutes | Serves 4

- 4 medium zucchinis, split in half
- ¼ cup olive oil
- 1 tbsp. kosher salt
- 1 tbsp. black pepper
- 1 cup grated Parmesan cheese
- ½ cup garlic chili oil

1. Season the zucchini with black pepper, salt and oil.
2. Place the cooking pot in the Ninja Foodi Smart XL Grill then set a grill grate inside.
3. Plug the thermometer into the appliance.
4. Place the cooking pot in the Ninja Foodi Smart XL Grill then set a grill grate inside.
5. Select the "Grill" Mode, set the temperature to MED.
6. Use the arrow keys to set the cooking time to 10 minutes.
7. Press the START/STOP button to initiate preheating.
8. Once preheated, place the zucchini in the Ninja Foodi Smart XL Grill.
9. Cover the hood and allow the grill to cook.
10. Flip the zucchini and add cheese on top and cover again then cook for 5 minutes.
11. Garnish with garlic chili oil.
12. Serve warm.

PER SERVING

Calories 361 | Fat 20g | Sodium 218mg | Carbs 16g | Fiber 10g | Sugar 30g | Protein 14g

Cheddar Bacon Corn

Prep time: 15 minutes | Cooking time: 12 minutes | Serves 10

- ½ cup butter, softened
- 1 packet ranch seasoning
- Black pepper, to taste
- 10 corn cobs
- 2 cups Cheddar, shredded
- 6 slices cooked bacon, crumbled
- Freshly chives, chopped
- Ranch, for drizzling

1. Mix butter with all the ingredients except the corn and cheese.
2. Place the cooking pot in the Ninja Foodi Smart XL Grill.
3. Select the Bake Mode and set the temperature to 350 degrees F.
4. Use the Arrow keys to set the time to 10 minutes.
5. Press the Start/Stop button to initiate preheating.
6. Once preheated, place the corn in the Ninja Foodi Smart XL Grill.
7. Cover the hood and allow the grill to cook.
8. Drizzle cheese on top and bake for 2 minutes.
9. Serve warm.

PER SERVING

Calories 391 | Fat 2.2g | Sodium 276mg | Carbs 27g | Fiber 0.9g | Sugar 1.4g | Protein 8.8g

Apple Salad

Prep time: 15 minutes | Cooking time: 10 minutes | Serves 4

- 6 tablespoons olive oil
- ¼ cup cilantro, minced
- ¼ cup vinegar
- 2 tablespoons honey
- 1 garlic clove, minced
- ¼ cup orange juice
- ½ teaspoon salt
- ½ teaspoon Sriracha chili sauce
- 2 large apples, wedged
- 1 pack (5 ounces) salad greens
- 1 cup walnut halves, toasted
- ½ cup crumbled Blue cheese

1. Place the cooking pot in the Ninja Foodi Smart XL Grill then place the grill grate in the pot.
2. Whisk the first eight ingredients in a bowl and add ¼ cup of this dressing to the apples.
3. Toss well and let them sit for 10 minutes.
4. Place the apples in the Ninja Foodi Smart XL Grill.
5. Cover the Ninja Foodi Smart XL Grill's Hood, select the Grill mode, set the temperature to LO and grill for 5 minutes per side.
6. Toss the rest of the salad ingredients together in a salad bowl.
7. Add grilled apples and serve.

PER SERVING

Calories 93 | Fat 3g | Sodium 510mg | Carbs 12g | Fiber 3g | Sugar 4g | Protein 4g

Sweet Grilled Pickles

Prep time: 15 minutes | Cooking time: 10 minutes | Serves 4

- Brine:
- 1 ¼ cup distilled white vinegar
- 1 ¼ cup water
- 1 cup sugar
- 2 tbsp. Kosher salt
- 2 tsp. crushed red pepper
- Pickles
- 5 large cucumbers, cut into 4 to 5-inch spears
- 1 white onion, sliced
- 6 sprigs dill
- 3 tsp. minced garlic
- 3 sanitized canning jars with lids

1. Place the cooking pot in the Ninja Foodi Smart XL Grill then set a grill grate inside.
2. Select the "Grill" Mode, set the temperature to MED.
3. Use the arrow keys to set the cooking time to 6 minutes.
4. Press the START/STOP button to initiate preheating.
5. Once preheated, place the cucumber in the Ninja Foodi Smart XL Grill.
6. Cover the hood and allow the grill to cook.
7. Flip the cucumber once cooked halfway through.
8. Mix the brine in a saucepan and divide into 2 canning jars.
9. Add 1 tsp. garlic and 2 dill sprigs to each jar.
10. Repeat the same steps with the onion.
11. Add cucumbers to one jar and onions to the other.
12. Close the lids and refrigerate them overnight.
13. Serve.

PER SERVING

Calories 318 | Fat 15.7g | Sodium 124mg | Carbs 27g | Fiber 0.1g | Sugar 0.3g | Protein 4.9g

Chapter 7
Snack and Side Recipes

Volcano Potatoes
Prep time: 15 minutes | Cooking time: 15 minutes | Serves 4

- 4 russet potatoes
- 8 strips bacon
- 1 cup cheddar cheese shredded
- Filling
- 2 cups cream cheese
- ½ green onion diced

1. Wrap the potatoes in a foil sheet.
2. Place the cooking pot in the Ninja Foodi Smart XL Grill then set a grill grate inside.
3. Select the "Bake" Mode, set the temperature to 400 degrees F.
4. Use the arrow keys to set the cooking time to 10 minutes.
5. Press the START/STOP button to initiate preheating.
6. Once preheated, place the potatoes in the Ninja Foodi Smart XL Grill.
7. Cover the hood and allow the grill to cook.
8. Allow the potatoes to cool, unwrap and scoop out the flesh from their center.
9. Mash the scooped out flesh in a bowl and stir in the rest of the except the bacon.
10. Stuff each potato shell with the mashed filling and wrap them with 2 bacon strips.
11. Once preheated, place the mixtures in the Ninja Foodi Smart XL Grill.
12. Cover the Ninja Foodi Smart XL Grill's hood, set the temperature to 350 degrees F and cook on the "BAKE Mode" for 10 minutes.
13. Drizzle cheese over the potatoes and broil for 5 minutes.
14. Serve warm.

PER SERVING

Calories 56 | Fat 4g | Sodium 634mg | Carbs 43g | Fiber 1.4g | Sugar 1g | Protein 13g

Ginger Salmon
Prep time: 15 minutes | Cooking time: 8 minutes | Serves 10

- 2 tablespoons rice vinegar
- 4 teaspoons sugar
- ½ teaspoon salt
- 1 tablespoon lime zest, grated
- ¼ cup lime juice
- 2 tablespoons olive oil
- ½ teaspoon ground coriander
- ½ teaspoon black pepper
- ⅓ cup fresh cilantro, chopped
- 1 tablespoon onion, chopped
- 2 teaspoons fresh ginger root, minced
- 2 garlic cloves, minced
- 2 medium cucumbers, peeled, seeded and chopped
- Salmon:
- ⅓ cup minced fresh gingerroot
- 1 tablespoon lime juice
- 1 tablespoon olive oil
- ½ teaspoon salt
- ½ teaspoon freshly ground pepper
- 10 (6 ounces) salmon fillets

1. Place the cooking pot in the Ninja Foodi Smart XL Grill then place the grill grate in the pot.
2. Start by blending the first 13 ingredients in a blender until smooth.
3. Season the salmon fillets with ginger, oil, salt, black pepper, lime juice.
4. Select the "Grill" Mode, set the temperature to MED.
5. Press the START/STOP button to initiate preheating.
6. Once preheated, place the fish fillets in the Ninja Foodi Smart XL Grill.
7. Cover the hood and allow the grill to cook for 6 minutes per side.
8. Cook the remaining fillets in a similar way.
9. Serve with the prepared sauce.

PER SERVING

Calories 376 | Fat 17g | Sodium 1127mg | Carbs 24g | Fiber 1g | Sugar 3g | Protein 29g

Crispy Rosemary Potatoes
Prep time: 10 minutes | Cooking time: 20 minutes | Serves 4

- 2 lb. baby red potatoes, quartered
- 2 tbsp. extra-virgin olive oil
- ¼ cup dried onion flakes
- 1 tsp. dried rosemary
- ½ tsp. onion powder
- ½ tsp. garlic powder
- ¼ tsp. celery
- ¼ tsp. freshly ground black pepper
- ½ tsp. dried parsley
- ½ tsp. sea salt

1. Insert the basket and close the hood. Select AIR FRYER, set the temperature to 390°F and set the time to 20 minutes.
2. Select START/STOP to start preheating.
3. Meanwhile, place all the ingredients in a large bowl and toss until evenly coated.
4. When the unit beeps to indicate it has preheated, add the potatoes to the basket.
5. Close the lid and cook for 10 minutes.
6. After 10 minutes, check for desired crispness.
7. Continue cooking up to 5 more minutes if necessary.

PER SERVING

Calories 232| Total Fat: 7g| Saturated Fat: 1g| Cholesterol: 0mg| Sodium: 249mg| Carbohydrates: 39g| Fiber: 6g| Protein: 4g

Baked Banana

Prep time: 10 minutes|Cooking time: 10 minutes|Serves 4

- 2 tbsp. dry shredded coconuts
- ¼ tsp. ground cinnamon
- 2 medium (7" to 7-7/8" long) bananas to be cut into bite-size pieces
- 1/3 cup dry breadcrumbs
- 1 tsp. white sugar
- 1 egg white

1. Preheat the Ninja Foodi Grill to 350°F (175°C).
2. Line the baking sheet with parchment paper.
3. Combine coconut, breadcrumbs, cinnamon and sugar in a bowl.
4. Beat egg white in a small bowl until it becomes frothy.
5. Dip each banana piece in egg white and press into the bread crumb mixture.
6. Then put the breaded bananas on the already prepared baking sheet.
7. Bake until it turns golden brown in about 10 minutes.

PER SERVING

Calories: 111.8| Carbohydrates: 20.8g| Protein: 3g| Fat: 2.6g| Sodium: 81.4mg

Pig Candy

Prep time: 10 minutes|Cooking time: 20 minutes|Serves 4

- ½ cup dark brown sugar
- ⅛ tsp. cayenne pepper
- 1 lb. thick cut bacon strips
- ¼ cup maple syrup

1. Mix cayenne pepper and brown sugar in a small bowl.
2. Drizzle this mixture over the bacon strips.
3. Place the cooking pot in the Ninja Foodi Smart XL Grill then set a grill grate inside.
4. Select the "Grill" Mode, set the temperature to MED.
5. Use the arrow keys on the display to select the cooking time to 10 minutes.
6. Press the START/STOP button to initiate preheating.
7. Once preheated, place the bacon in the Ninja Foodi Smart XL Grill.
8. Cover the hood and allow the grill to cook.
9. Brush the bacon with maple syrup and cook for 10 minutes more.
10. Serve.

PER SERVING

Calories 85 | Fat 8g |Sodium 146mg | Carbs 25g | Fiber 0.1g | Sugar 0.4g | Protein 1g

Basil Shrimp Appetizer

Prep time: 5-10 minutes|Cooking time: 8 minutes|Serves 4-6

- 2 tsp. olive oil
- Black pepper (ground) and salt to taste
- 1-lb. shrimp, peeled and deveined
- 1 tbsp. basil, chopped

1. Take a Ninja Foodi Grill, arrange it over a cooking platform and open the top lid.
2. In the unit, place the basket. Add all the and combine them.
3. Select the "Air Fryer" mode and adjust the 370°F temperature level. Then, set the timer to 8 minutes and press "STOP/START," which will start the cooking process.
4. When the timer goes off, open the lid. Serve it warm.

PER SERVING

Calories: 117| Fat: 5g| Saturated Fat: 1g| Trans Fat: 0g| Carbohydrates: 2g| Fiber: 0g| Sodium: 924mg| Protein: 15g

Bison Sliders

Prep time: 10 minutes|Cooking time: 12 minutes|Serves 4

- 1 lb. ground buffalo meat
- 3 garlic cloves minced
- 2 tbsp. Worcestershire sauce
- 1 tsp. kosher salt
- 1 tsp. black pepper
- Cheese slices
- For Serving
- Green onion thinly sliced
- Yellow mustard
- Tomato ketchup
- Lettuce
- Pickles

1. Mix meat with black pepper, salt and Worcestershire sauce in a large bowl.
2. Make 8 patties out of this mixture.
3. Place the cooking pot in the Ninja Foodi Smart XL Grill then set a grill grate inside.
4. Select the "Grill" Mode, set the temperature to MED.
5. Use the arrow keys to set the cooking time to 10 minutes.
6. Press the START/STOP button to initiate preheating.
7. Once preheated, place the patties in the Ninja Foodi Smart XL Grill.
8. Cover the hood and allow the grill to cook.
9. Grill the buns for 2 minutes per side.
10. Add each patty in between the two sides of the buns and add other veggies to the buns.
11. Serve warm.

PER SERVING

Calories 24 | Fat 1g |Sodium 236mg | Carbs 22g | Fiber 0.3g | Sugar 0.1g | Protein 31g

Lovely Seasonal Broccoli

Prep time: 10 minutes|Cooking time: 10 minutes|Serves 4

- ½ tsp salt
- ½ tsp red chili powder
- ¼ tsp spice mix
- 2 tbsp yogurt
- 1 tablespoon chickpea flour
- ¼ tsp turmeric powder
- 1 pound broccoli, cut into florets

1. Take your florets and wash them thoroughly.
2. Take a bowl and add listed , except the florets.
3. Add broccoli and combine the mix well; let the mixture sit for 30 minutes.
4. Pre-heat your Ninja Foodi Smart XL Grill to "AIR CRISP" mode at 390 degrees F and set the timer to 10 minutes.
5. Once you hear a beep, add florets to Crisper Basket and crisp for 10 minutes.

PER SERVING

Calories: 111|Fat: 2 g| Carbohydrates: 12 g| Fiber: 1 g| Sodium: 024 mg| Protein: 7 g

Mayonnaise Corn

Prep time: 5-10 minutes| Cooking time: 14 minutes|Serves 3-4

- ¼ cup sour cream
- ¼ cup mayonnaise
- 3 ears corn, husked, rinsed and dried
- Olive oil spray
- ½ tsp. garlic powder
- ¼ tsp. chili powder
- ¼ cup crumbled cotija cheese
- 1 tsp. freshly squeezed lime juice
- Fresh cilantro leaves, for garnish
- ½ tsp. salt
- ½ tsp. Black pepper (ground)

1. Take the Ninja Foodi Grill, arrange it over a cooking platform and open the top lid.
2. In the unit, place the basket and coat it with some cooking spray. In the basket, add the corn and close the lid.
3. Select the "AIR FRYER" mode and adjust the 400°F temperature level. Then, set the timer to 12 minutes and press "STOP/START," which will start the cooking process. Shake the basket after 6 minutes.
4. In a mixing bowl, stir together the sour cream, mayonnaise, cheese, lime juice, garlic powder and chili powder.
5. Add the cream mixture over the corn. Season to taste with salt and black pepper. Top with cilantro and more chili powder.

PER SERVING

Calories: 265| Fat: 13.5g| Saturated Fat: 5g| Trans Fat: 0g| Carbohydrates: 29g| Fiber: 4g| Sodium: 687mg| Protein: 7.5g

Grilled Peach Salsa

Prep time: 15 minutes|Cooking time: 10 minutes|Serves 4

- 4 peaches, halved and pitted
- 4 heirloom tomatoes diced
- 1 bunch cilantro
- 2 limes juiced
- 2 garlic cloves minced
- 2 tbsp. olive oil
- Sea salt to taste
- Black pepper to taste

1. Brush the peaches with oil.
2. Place the cooking pot in the Ninja Foodi Smart XL Grill then set a grill grate inside.
3. Select the "Grill" Mode, set the temperature to MED.
4. Use the arrow keys to set the cooking time to 10 minutes.
5. Press the START/STOP button to initiate preheating.
6. Once preheated, place the fruits in the Ninja Foodi Smart XL Grill.
7. Cover the hood and allow the grill to cook.
8. Dice the grilled peaches and mix with rest of the in a bowl.
9. Serve.

PER SERVING

Calories 82 | Fat 6g |Sodium 620mg | Carbs 25g | Fiber 2.4g | Sugar 1.2g | Protein 12g

Grilled Butternut Squash

Prep time: 15 minutes| Cooking time: 16 minutes|Serves 4

- 1 medium butternut squash
- 1 tablespoon olive oil
- 1 ½ teaspoons dried oregano
- 1 teaspoon dried thyme
- ½ teaspoon salt
- ¼ teaspoon black pepper

1. Place the cooking pot in the Ninja Foodi Smart XL Grill then place the grill grate in the pot.
2. Peel and slice the squash into ½ inch thick slices.
3. Remove the center of the slices to discard the seeds.
4. Toss the squash slices with the remaining in a bowl.
5. Plug the thermometer into the appliance.
6. Select the "Grill" Mode, set the temperature to MED.
7. Use the arrow keys to set the time to 16 minutes.
8. Press the START/STOP button to initiate preheating.
9. Place the squash in the Ninja Foodi Smart XL Grill.
10. Cover the hood and allow the grill to cook.
11. Serve warm.

PER SERVING

Calories 180 | Fat 9g | Sodium 318mg | Carbs 19g | Fiber 5g | Sugar 3g | Protein 7g

Grilled Kimchi

Prep time: 20 minutes | Cooking time: 6 minutes | Serves 4

- ½ cup kochukaru
- 2 tsp. sauejeot
- 1 napa cabbage, cut into 2 inch pieces
- 8 oz daikon radish
- ½ cup kosher salt
- 4 medium scallions end trimmed, cut into 1-inch-long pieces
- ¼ cup fish sauce
- ¼ cup minced ginger
- 1 tbsp. of minced garlic cloves
- 1½ tsp. granulated sugar

1. Toss cabbage with salt and soak in water for 12 hours then drain.
2. Place the cooking pot in the Ninja Foodi Smart XL Grill then set a Crisper Basket inside.
3. Plug the thermometer into the unit and place it inside the pot.
4. Select the "Air Crisp" Mode, set the temperature to 400 degrees F.
5. Use the arrow keys to set the cooking time to 6 minutes.
6. Press the START/STOP button to initiate preheating.
7. Once preheated, place the cabbage in the Ninja Foodi Smart XL Grill.
8. Mix other ingredients in a bowl and stir in cabbage pieces then cover and refrigerate for 12 hours.
9. Serve.

PER SERVING

Calories 132 | Fat 10g | Sodium 994mg | Carbs 13g | Fiber 0.4g | Sugar 3g | Protein 8g

Grilled Stuffed Mushrooms

Prep time: 10 minutes | Cooking time: 10 minutes | Serves 8

- 8 portobello mushrooms
- cheddar cheese grated or shredded
- Filling
- 4 slices bacon
- ½ lb. cream cheese
- 1 large red onion sliced
- 1 jalapeño peppers liked

1. Sear bacon slices in a skillet until crispy and keep them aside.
2. Mix jalapenos, cream cheese, bacon, and onion in a small bowl.
3. Stuff each mushroom with this cream cheese mixture.
4. Place the cooking pot in the Ninja Foodi Smart XL Grill then set a grill grate inside.
5. Select the "Grill" Mode, set the temperature to MED.
6. Use the arrow keys to set the cooking time to 10 minutes.
7. Press the START/STOP button to initiate preheating.
8. Once preheated, place the mushrooms in the Ninja Foodi Smart XL Grill.
9. Cover the hood and allow the grill to cook.
10. Drizzle cheese on top of the mushrooms and bake for 5 minutes.
11. Serve warm.

PER SERVING

Calories 449 | Fat 31g | Sodium 723mg | Carbs 22g | Fiber 2.5g | Sugar 2g | Protein 26g

Air Fryer Avocado Fries

Prep time: 10 minutes | Cooking time: 5 minutes | Serves 2

- ¼ cup all-purpose flour
- ¼ tsp. salt
- 1 tsp. water
- ½ cup panko breadcrumbs
- ½ tsp. ground black pepper
- 1 egg
- 1 ripe avocado, should be halved, seeded, and peeled before cutting into 8 slices
- 1 serving cooking spray

1. Select Air Fryer and Preheat the Ninja Foodi Grill to about 400°F (200°C).
2. Mix the pepper, flour and salt in a shallow bowl.
3. Get another shallow bowl and beat water and egg together in it.
4. Then put panko in a third shallow bowl.
5. Dredge an avocado slice through the flour, but you should shake off any excess.
6. Dip into the egg and let the excess fall off.
7. Finally, press the slice into the panko so that both sides are well covered.
8. Set it on a plate and repeat this process with the remaining slices.
9. Spray avocado slices generously with cooking spray and arrange them in the Ninja Foodi basket, they should be sprayed side-down. Spray the top part of the avocado slices also.
10. Cook in the already preheated Ninja Foodi for about 4 minutes.
11. Turn the avocado slices over and cook until they become golden in about 3 minutes.

PER SERVING

Calories: 319 | Carbohydrates: 39.8g | Protein: 9.3g | Fat: 18g | Cholesterol: 81.8mg | Sodium: 452.9mg

Figs Stuffed with Cheese
Prep time: 10 minutes | Cooking time: 10 minutes | Serves 10

- 20 ripe figs
- 4 oz soft goat cheese
- 2 tbsp. olive oil
- 2 tbsp. balsamic vinegar
- 1 tbsp. fresh rosemary, chopped

1. Cut a cross on top (about ¾ way down) of each fig.
2. Mix goat cheese, oil, vinegar and rosemary in a bowl.
3. Stuff each fig with the goat cheese mixture.
4. Place the cooking pot in the Ninja Foodi Smart XL Grill then set a grill grate inside.
5. Select the "Grill" Mode, set the temperature to LOW.
6. Use the arrow keys to set the cooking time to 10 minutes.
7. Press the START/STOP button to initiate preheating.
8. Once preheated, place the figs in the Ninja Foodi Smart XL Grill.
9. Cover the hood and allow the grill to cook.
10. Serve.

PER SERVING

Calories 38 | Fat 7g | Sodium 316mg | Carbs 24g | Fiber 0.3g | Sugar 0.3g | Protein 3g

Grilled Potato Wedges
Prep time: 10 minutes | Cooking time: 20 minutes | Serves 6

- 6 russet potatoes medium-sized, cut into wedges
- ½ cup cooking oil
- 2 tbsp. paprika
- ¼ cup salt
- 1 tbsp. black pepper
- ⅔ cup potato flakes

1. Toss potato wedges with black pepper and other in a bowl.
2. Place the cooking pot in the Ninja Foodi Smart XL Grill then set a grill grate inside.
3. Select the "Grill" Mode, set the temperature to MED.
4. Use the arrow keys to set the cooking time to 10 minutes.
5. Press the START/STOP button to initiate preheating.
6. Once preheated, place the mushrooms in the Ninja Foodi Smart XL Grill.
7. Cover the hood and allow the grill to cook.
8. Serve warm.

PER SERVING

Calories 218 | Fat 14g | Sodium 220mg | Carbs 22g | Fiber 2.4g | Sugar 1.2g | Protein 2.5g

Cob with Pepper Butter
Prep time: 15 minutes | Cooking time: 15 minutes | Serves 8

- 8 medium ears sweet corn
- 1 cup butter, softened
- 2 tablespoons lemon-pepper seasoning

1. Place the cooking pot in the Ninja Foodi Smart XL Grill then place the grill grate in the pot.
2. Season the corn cob with butter and lemon pepper liberally.
3. Place the corn cob in the Ninja Foodi Smart XL Grill.
4. Cover the Ninja Foodi Smart XL Grill's Hood, select the Grill mode, select the Low setting and grill for 15 minutes with grilling after every 5 minutes.
5. Grill the corn cobs in batches.
6. Serve warm.

PER SERVING

Calories 218 | Fat 22g | Sodium 350mg | Carbs 32.2g | Fiber 0.7g | Sugar 1g | Protein 4.3g

Tarragon Asparagus
Prep time: 15 minutes | Cooking time: 8 minutes | Serves 4

- 2 pounds fresh asparagus, trimmed
- 2 tablespoons olive oil
- 1 teaspoon salt
- ½ teaspoon black pepper
- ¼ cup honey
- 4 tablespoons fresh tarragon, minced

1. Place the cooking pot in the Ninja Foodi Smart XL Grill then place the grill grate in the pot.
2. Liberally season the asparagus by tossing it with oil, salt, pepper, honey and tarragon.
3. Select the "Grill" Mode, set the temperature to MED.
4. Press the START/STOP button to initiate preheating.
5. Place the asparagus in the Ninja Foodi Smart XL Grill.
6. Cover the hood and allow the grill to cook for 4 minutes per side.
7. Serve warm.

PER SERVING

Calories 104 | Fat 3g | Sodium 216mg | Carbs 17g | Fiber 3g | Sugar 4g | Protein 1g

Chapter 8
Bonus

Peach BBQ Chicken Thighs

Prep time: 15 minutes|Cooking time: 15 minutes|Serves 6

- 4- 6 chicken thighs bone-in
- ¾ cup barbecue sauce
- 4 Tbsp peach preserve
- 1½ Tbsp Lemon Juice
- Salt and Pepper to taste

1. Start by mixing peach preserves, barbecue sauce, lemon juice, and salt and pepper in a bowl. Whisk until well incorporated.
2. Place your chicken thighs in the marinade for 4 hours at a minimum.
3. Once chicken is done marinating, select GRILL mode and adjust the temperature to HI and preheat your Ninja Foodi Grill for 10 minutes. Toss chicken thighs on the grill, skin down.
4. Cook 4-5 minutes per side or until the chicken is nice and brown. Once get a nice grill mark on them, drop the heat down to medium.
5. Then finish cooking until the chicken reaches an internal temperature of 165 degrees F.
6. Remove chicken and place on a plate, and lightly cover with aluminum foil.
7. Let chicken rest 5 minutes before serving.

PER SERVING

Calories 342| Carbohydrates 15g | Protein 31g | Fat 18g | Sodium 639mg| Fiber 0g

Grilled Huli Huli Chicken

Prep time: 5 minutes|Cooking time: 12 minutes|Serves 8

- 6-8 Chicken Legs
- ½ tsp fresh ginger, minced or crushed
- 1 tsp garlic, minced or crushed
- ¼ cup brown sugar
- 3 Tbsp ketchup
- 4 Tbsp soy sauce
- 2 Tbsp chicken stock, as needed

1. In a bowl, add ketchup, soy sauce, garlic, ginger, and brown sugar.
2. Mix well and slowly add in the chicken stock. thin up the marinade a bit to make it easier to cover the chicken.
3. In a container or bag add your chicken legs and pour ½ of the marinade sauce all over the chicken.
4. Cover and let marinate at least 2 hours to overnight.
5. Once the chicken is marinated, preheat your Ninja Foodi Grill or another grill after selecting the GRILL mode at HIGH heat.
6. When it hot toss your chicken legs on, leaving space between each.
7. Cook 4-6 minutes on each side, basting with the remaining marinade.
8. Cook until the internal temperature reaches 165 degrees F internal temperature.
9. Remove the Huli Huli chicken from the grill, let the rest 5 minutes then serve with your favorite sides.

PER SERVING

Calories 509 | Carbohydrates 8g | Protein 63g | Fat 23g | Sodium 752mg| Fiber 0g

Beer Bratwurst

Prep time: 15 minutes|Cooking time: 8 minutes|Serves 4

- 2 lbs. boneless pork shoulder, cut into cubes
- ⅔ lb. boneless veal shoulder, cut into cubes
- ½ cup pale ale
- 1 tbsp. fine sea salt
- 1 tsp. sugar
- 1 tsp. caraway seeds
- ½ tsp. dry mustard powder
- 1 tsp. fresh thyme leaves
- ½ tsp. ground ginger
- ¼ tsp. freshly grated nutmeg
- Hog casings, rinsed

1. Mix nutmeg, ginger, thyme, mustard powder, caraway seeds, sugar and salt in a small bowl.
2. Grind the pork meat in a food processor then add semi frozen ale.
3. Stir in spice mixture, mix well and take 2 tbsp. of the beef mixture to make a sausage.
4. Make more sausages and keep them aside.
5. Place the cooking pot in the Ninja Foodi Smart XL Grill then set a grill grate inside.
6. Select the "Grill" Mode, set the temperature to MED.
7. Press the START/STOP button to initiate preheating.
8. Once preheated, place the pork in the Ninja Foodi Smart XL Grill.
9. Cover the hood and allow the grill to cook for 8 minutes, flipping halfway through.
10. Serve warm.

PER SERVING

Calories 384 | Fat 25g |Sodium 460mg | Carbs 16g | Fiber 0.4g | Sugar 2g | Protein 26g

Chicken Roast with Pineapple Salsa

Prep time: 10 minutes | Cooking time: 45 minutes | Serves 2

- ¼ cup extra virgin olive oil
- ¼ cup freshly chopped cilantro
- 1 red bell pepper
- 1 red onion
- 1-lb. boneless chicken breasts
- 2 cup pineapples
- 2 tsp. honey
- Juice from 1 lime
- Salt and pepper to taste

1. Insert the basket and close the lid.
2. Select AIR FRYER, set the temperature to 390°F and the time to 45 minutes. Select START/STOP to start preheating.
3. Place the grill pan accessory in the air fryer.
4. Combine pineapple, red pepper, red onion, cilantro, lime juice and salt in a small bowl for the salsa. Set it aside.
5. Season the chicken breasts with lime juice, olive oil, honey, salt and pepper.
6. Arrange the chicken over the Air Fryer and cook it.
7. Top the chicken with sauce and serve.

PER SERVING

Calories: 744 | Fat: 33g | Protein: 5g | Sugar: 5g

Grilled Chicken Bruschetta

Prep time: 10 minutes | Cooking time: 15 minutes | Serves 3

- 3 Chicken Breasts
- Roasted Garlic and Bell Pepper Seasoning
- Salt and Pepper, to taste
- Cooking Oil Spray for Grill
- 1 cup Basil Pesto
- Fresh Mozzarella Cheese, Sliced
- 2 Roma Tomatoes, diced

1. Place the chicken in gallon size bag and then use a meat mallet to pound the chicken to around ¼" thick.
2. Remove from bag and place raw chicken on a platter and season with the Roasted Garlic and Bell Pepper Seasoning.
3. For the Ninja Foodi Grill, select the AIR CRISP setting and adjust the temperature to 400 degrees F.
4. Grill the chicken for 15 minutes, while cooking after 5 minutes, place some pesto on top of each chicken breast, then slice and lay out some fresh mozzarella on each slice of chicken.
5. Remove your grilled bruschetta chicken from the Ninja Foodi Grill and top with diced roma tomatoes, add extra pesto, basil leaves and serve as desired.

PER SERVING

Calories 359 | Carbohydrates 6g | Protein 25g | Fat 5g | Sodium 399mg | Fiber 1g

Chicken & Bacon Caesar Salad

Prep time: 35 minutes | Cooking time: 30 minutes | Serves 4

- Marinated Chicken Breasts
- 1 lb chicken breasts
- ⅛ cup balsamic vinegar
- ⅛ cup olive oil
- ¼ tsp garlic powder
- ¼ tsp black pepper
- ¼ tsp salt
- Caesar Dressing
- ⅔ cup mayo
- 4 anchovies in oil
- 2 small cloves garlic
- 2.5 tbsp lemon juice
- 2 tbsp nutritional yeast
- ½ tsp dijon mustard
- ½ tsp coconut amino
- ¼ tsp apple cider vinegar
- ½ tsp salt
- ¼ tsp pepper
- Salad & Toppings
- 8 cups romaine lettuce
- 8 oz. sugar free bacon cooked
- 1 tsp nutritional yeast

1. Prepare the Chicken Breasts: Put one chicken breast inside a zip lock bag Gently pound the chicken using a meat tenderizer or heavy rolling pin until it's even in thickness.
2. Repeat for the other chicken breasts.
3. Whisk together the marinade ingredients and pour it over the chicken, turning to coat. Marinate for 30-60 minutes.
4. Select the GRILL function of the Ninja Foodi Grill and adjust the temperature to MEDIUM and preheat.
5. Turn your grill to medium and allow preheating.
6. Add the chicken breasts to the grill, cooking for about 12 minutes, turning once.
7. Remove from the heat and let the chicken on the rest before slicing.
8. Prepare the Salad Toppings: Wash and chop the lettuce.
9. Cook the bacon and allow it to cool, and then roughly chop it.
10. Boil the eggs however you like them and slice them into halves or quarters.
11. Make the Caesar Salad Dressing: Using an immersion blender set to low, mix together all the ingredients, smash the garlic clove and finely chop the anchovies, then whisk all ingredients together in a bowl.
12. Season to taste with salt and pepper.
13. Keep it covered in the refrigerator for up to 5 days.
14. Assemble the Salad: Divide the lettuce among four large bowls.
15. Sprinkle each salad with cracked black pepper and enjoy.

PER SERVING

Calories 631 | Carbohydrates 12g | Protein 42g | Fat 46g | Sodium 1461mg | Fiber 3g

Orange Curried Chicken
Prep time: 15 minutes|Cooking time: 45 minutes|Serves 4

- ¼ cup orange marmalade
- 1 tsp. salt
- ½ cup water
- 1 tsp. curry powder
- 4 bone-in chicken breast, with skin

1. Preheat the unit to 350°F.
2. In a small bowl, combine the marmalade, curry, salt and water.
3. Put the chicken in the pan, insert it in the unit.
4. Select Bake and close the lid. Cook for 45 minutes, spooning sauce over the chicken several times.
5. Serve it warm.

PER SERVING

Calories: 589| Fat: 21g| Protein: 47,4g

Honey-Mustard Chicken Tenders
Prep time: 5 minutes|Cooking time: 8 minutes|Serves 4

- ½ cup Dijon mustard
- 2 tbsp. honey
- 2 tbsp. olive oil
- 1 tsp. freshly ground black pepper
- 2 lb. chicken tenders
- ½ cup walnuts

1. Whisk together the mustard, honey, olive oil and pepper in a medium bowl.
2. Add the chicken and toss to coat.
3. Finely grind the walnuts by pulsing them in a food processor or putting them in a heavy-duty plastic bag and pounding them with a rolling pin or heavy skillet.
4. Insert the Grill Grate and close the lid. Select GRILL, set the temperature to HIGH, and the time to 8 minutes.
5. Select START/STOP to start preheating.
6. Then arrange the chicken over the grill grate and cook it.
7. Serve it with walnut crumbs.

PER SERVING

Calories: 444| Fat: 20g| Protein: 5g

Air Fryer Chicken Fajitas
Prep time: 35 minutes|Cooking time: 15 minutes|Serves 4

- 1 tbsp. extra-virgin olive oil
- 4 boneless, skinless chicken breasts, sliced
- ¼ lime juice
- 1 small red onion, sliced
- 2 red peppers flakes
- Tortillas, for serving
- 2 cup torn butter lettuce
- Salt and pepper

1. In a large bowl, mix together oil, lime juice, red pepper flakes.
2. Season chicken with salt and pepper. Let to marinate for 30 minutes.
3. Insert the basket and close the lid. Select AIR FRYER, set the temperature to 165°F and the time to 15 minutes. Select START/STOP to start preheating.
4. Place the chicken, onion and pepper in the air fryer basket.
5. Cook and serve with lettuce and tortillas.

PER SERVING

Calories: 783| Fat: 38g| Protein: 72g| Fiber: 12g

Chili-Spiced Ribs
Prep time: 15 minutes|Cooking time: 50 minutes|Serves 6

- Glaze:
- 1 cup of soy sauce
- 1 cup packed brown sugar
- ⅔ cup ketchup
- ⅓ cup lemon juice
- 1 ½ teaspoon fresh ginger root, minced
- Ribs:
- 6 pounds pork baby back ribs
- 3 tablespoons packed brown sugar
- 2 tablespoons paprika
- 2 tablespoons chili powder
- 3 teaspoons ground cumin
- 2 teaspoons garlic powder
- 1 teaspoon salt

1. Take the first six ingredients in a suitable bowl and mix well.
2. Place the cooking pot in the Ninja Foodi Smart XL Grill then place the grill grate in the pot.
3. Plug the thermometer into the appliance.
4. Select the "Grill" Mode, set the temperature to MAX then select the PRESET.
5. Use the right arrow keys on the display to select "BEEF" and set the doneness to MED WELL.
6. Press the START/STOP button to initiate preheating.
7. Place the ribs in the Ninja Foodi Smart XL Grill.
8. Insert the thermometer probe into the thickest part of the ribs.
9. Cover the hood and allow the grill to cook.
10. Meanwhile, prepare the sauce by cooking its for eight minutes in a saucepan.
11. Pour this sauce over the grilled ribs in the Ninja Foodi Smart XL Grill.
12. Grill for another 5 minutes per side.
13. Serve.

PER SERVING

Calories 305 | Fat 25g | Sodium 532mg | Carbs 2.3g | Fiber 0.4g | Sugar 2g | Protein 18.3g

Tarragon Chicken Tenders

Prep time: 5 minutes | Cooking time: 8 minutes | Serves 4

- For The Chicken:
- 1½ lb. chicken tenders (12 to 16 tenders)
- Coarse salt (kosher or sea and freshly ground black pepper
- 3 tbsp. chopped fresh tarragon leaves, plus 4 whole sprigs for garnish
- 1 tsp. finely grated lemon zest
- 2 tbsp. fresh lemon juice
- 2 tbsp. extra-virgin olive oil
- For The Sauce (Optional):
- 2 tbsp. fresh lemon juice
- 2 tbsp. salted butter
- ½ cup heavy (whipping cream)

1. Make the chicken: Place the chicken tenders in a nonreactive baking dish just large enough to hold them in a single layer.
2. Season the tenders generously on both sides with salt and pepper.
3. Sprinkle the chopped tarragon and lemon zest all over the tenders, patting them onto the chicken with your fingertips.
4. Drizzle the lemon juice and the olive oil over the tenders and pat them onto the chicken.
5. Let the tenders marinate in the refrigerator, covered, for 10 minutes.
6. Drain the chicken tenders well by lifting one end with tongs and letting the marinade drip off.
7. Discard the marinade.
8. Insert the Grill Grate and close the hood.
9. Select GRILL, set the temperature to HIGH and set the time to 8 minutes.
10. Select START/STOP to start preheating.
11. Then arrange the chicken over the grill and cook it.
12. Serve it with sauce.

PER SERVING

Calories: 299 | Fat: 20g | Protein: 52g

Minted Tomato, Onion & Glazed Tofu Kebabs

Prep time: 15 minutes | Cooking time: 40 minutes | Serves 4

- 1 14-ounce package extra-firm water-packed tofu, drained
- 1 tablespoon lime juice
- 16 fresh mint leaves
- 4 plum tomatoes, quartered and seeded
- 1 tablespoon reduced-sodium soy sauce
- 1 tsp minced fresh ginger
- 1 onion, peeled, quartered and separated into layers
- 2 jalapeño peppers, seeded and cut into ½-inch pieces
- ¼ cup Kecap manis

1. Insert Grill Grate. Select the GRILL mode, adjust temperature to LOW and time to 10 minutes. Preheat the Ninja Foodi Grill..
2. Cut the tofu in half horizontally, cutting 2 large slices about one inch thick.
3. Take a kitchen towel and put it on the cutting board.
4. Set the tofu on the towel.
5. Put another clean folded towel over the tofu.
6. Put a flat and heavyweight thing like a skillet on top; Drain it for 15 minutes; then remove the weight and cut the tofu into 1½-inch pieces.
7. Combine the lime juice, soy sauce, and ginger in a bowl.
8. Add the tofu and toss it to coat.
9. Cover it and marinate in the refrigerator for 15 minutes.
10. Tuck in a mint leaf into every tomato quarter and thread them onto four or 8 skewers alternatively with onion, tofu, and jalapenos.
11. Add the food to the Grill Grate and close the hood.
12. Cook for 10 minutes.

PER SERVING

Calories 412 | Carbohydrates 64.3g | Protein 16.1g | Fat 10.1g | Sodium 895mg | Fiber 2g

Grilled Pork Chops with Pineapple Glaze

Prep time: 10 minutes | Cooking time: 14 minutes | Serves 4

- ½ cup pineapple juice
- ¼ cup honey
- ¼ cup unseasoned rice vinegar
- 3 tbsp. Dijon mustard
- 1 tsp. crushed red pepper flakes
- ½ tsp. toasted sesame oil
- ½ tsp. ground turmeric
- 4 (1"-thick) bone-in pork chops
- Kosher salt, to taste

1. Mix pineapple juice, honey, rice vinegar, mustard, red pepper flakes, sesame oil and turmeric in a bowl.
2. Mix the pork chops with the marinade in a shallow tray, cover and refrigerate for 30 minutes.
3. Place the cooking pot in the Ninja Foodi Smart XL Grill then set a grill grate inside.
4. Plug the thermometer into the appliance.
5. Select the "Grill" Mode, set the temperature to MED then select the PRESET.
6. Use the right arrow keys on the display to select "PORK" and set the doneness to MED WELL.
7. Press the START/STOP button to initiate preheating.
8. Once preheated, place the pork in the Ninja Foodi Smart XL Grill.
9. Insert the thermometer probe into the thickest part of the pork.
10. Cover the hood and allow the grill to cook.
11. Serve warm.

PER SERVING

Calories 419 | Fat 13g | Sodium 432mg | Carbs 19g | Fiber 3g | Sugar 1g | Protein 33g

Marinated London Broil
Prep time: 5 minutes | Cooking time: 8 minutes | Serves 4

- 1½ lbs London Broil
- ¼ cup red wine vinegar
- 1 Tbsp olive oil
- 1½ Tbsp spicy mustard
- 2 cloves garlic minced
- 1 Tbsp Worcestershire sauce
- 1-2 tsp rosemary fresh
- 1 tsp sea salt
- 1 tsp onion powder
- 1 tsp dried thyme
- ½ tsp black pepper

1. Tenderize each side with a meat tenderizer.
2. Mince the garlic cloves and finely chop the rosemary. Combine all the marinade ingredients into a large plastic, sealable bag. Add the steak and seal the bag. Mix the marinade all around so the ingredients combine with each other. Then squeeze the air out of the bag and refrigerate for 2-4 hours.
3. Remove the steak from the fridge, leave it in the bag and let it sit at room temp for 30 minutes.
4. Remove the steak from the bag and blot off the marinade.
5. Select GRILL mode, adjust the temperature to MAX heat and preheat. When it says "ADD FOOD" lays the steak on the grill surface and presses the steak down onto the grill surface.
6. Grill on max grill for 4 minutes and then flip. Grill on max grill another 2-4 minutes for medium rare. Remove from grill and let the steak rest for 5-10 minutes.

PER SERVING

Calories 265 | Carbohydrates 2g | Protein 40g | Fat 9g | Sodium 798mg | Fiber 1g

Carne Asada Street Tacos
Prep time: 3 minutes | Cooking time: 20 minutes | Serves 8

- 2 tsp sea salt
- 2 tsp cumin
- 2 tsp smoked paprika
- 1 tsp garlic powder
- 1 tsp onion powder
- ¼ tsp chipotle
- ½ cup orange juice fresh squeezed
- ¼ cup lime juice
- 4 garlic cloves about ½ Tbsp
- 1 Ancho chili pepper dry
- 1 cup cilantro I use the stems
- Carne Asada
- 1½ pounds skirt steak
- 1 cup beef stock
- 16 corn tortillas
- 4 ounces cotija cheese
- Cilantro for garnish
- ½ cup radishes sliced.
- 1 cup onion diced

1. Mix up the spices and add to a medium size sealable bag.
2. Slice the steak against the grain into thin strips and place into baggy with the dry spices. Shake to coat meat and then add the remaining marinade ingredients. Leave at room temp for 30 minutes or refrigerate for 4 hours or overnight.
3. Dump the steak and the marinade into the inner pot. Add 1 cup of beef stock. Set the pressure on high for 10 minutes.
4. Allow the Ninja Foodi to release its pressure for 10 minutes then immediately release the remaining pressure.
5. Select the "Air Crisp" function of the Ninja Foodi Grill at 360 Degrees F for 5 minutes.
6. Put the rack in the high position and lay the corn tortillas over 2 rungs in the rack. Spritzing with oil will help them be more pliable.
7. Air Crisp the Tortillas for 3 minutes or until they become warm and slightly crispy.
8. Double the corn tortillas and stuff with carne a Sada meat and top with crumbled cheese, cilantro, onion, and sliced radishes.
9. Serve & Enjoy!

PER SERVING

Calories 308 | Carbohydrates 34g | Protein 24g | Fat 9g | Sodium 731mg | Fiber 5g

Juicy Stuffed Bell Peppers
Prep time: 10 minutes | Cooking time: 15 minutes | Serves 4

- 4 slices bacon, cooked and chopped
- 4 large eggs
- 1 cup cheddar cheese, shredded
- 4 bell peppers, seeded and tops removed
- Chopped parsley for garnish
- Salt and pepper to taste

1. Divide cheese and bacon equally and stuff into your bell pepper.
2. Add eggs into each bell pepper. Season with salt and pepper.
3. Pre-heat your Ninja Foodi by pressing the "AIR CRISP" option and setting it to "390 Degrees F."
4. Set the timer to 15 minutes.
5. Let it pre-heat until you hear a beep.
6. Transfer bell pepper to your cooking basket and transfer to Ninja Foodi Grill.
7. Lock lid and cook for 10-15 minutes.
8. Cook until egg whites are cooked well until the yolks are slightly runny.
9. Remove peppers from the basket and garnish with parsley.
10. Serve and enjoy!

PER SERVING

Calories 326 | Carbohydrates 10g | Protein 22g | Fat 23g | Sodium 781mg | Fiber 2g

Chicken Satay

Prep time: 40 minutes | Cooking time: 6 minutes | Serves 3

- 1½ lbs chicken breast boneless, skinless
- Marinade
- ½ cup coconut milk
- 2 cloves garlic minced
- 2" piece ginger grated
- 2 tsp turmeric
- 1 tsp sea salt
- 1 Tbsp Lemongrass Paste
- 1 Tbsp Chili Garlic Sauce
- 2 tsp Lemon Juice
- Optional Garnishes
- chopped cilantro
- chopped peanuts
- peanut sauce

1. If using bamboo skewers, soak them in water for at least 30 minutes before using.
2. Mix all the ingredients in the marinade in a medium size bowl.
3. Slice chicken breast into ½" strips and place into the marinade. Allow to marinate at room temp for 30 minutes.
4. Turn the Ninja Foodi Grill on and select the GRILL function and MAX temp. Make sure the Grill Grate that came with the grill is inside during the preheat. While the NF preheats, assemble your chicken skewers.
5. Take a strip and weave it onto a skewer.
6. When the Ninja Foodi Grill has preheated it will tell you to "ADD FOOD." Add about 6 skewers to the Grill Grate surface. Add more if they will fit, but don't overlap them or they won't cook evenly.
7. Close the lid and set the time for 6 minutes. Grill for 3 minutes and flip the skewers. Grill an additional 2-3 minutes
8. Garnish with fresh cilantro and chopped peanuts.

PER SERVING

Calories 177 | Carbohydrates 3g | Protein 25g | Fat 75g | Sodium 622mg | Fiber 1g

Moroccan Roast Chicken

Prep time: 5-10 minutes | Cooking time: 22 minutes | Serves 4

- 3 tbsp plain yogurt
- 4 skinless, boneless chicken thighs
- 4 garlic cloves, chopped
- ½ tsp salt
- ⅓ cup olive oil
- ½ tsp fresh flat-leaf parsley, chopped
- 2 tsp ground cumin
- 2 tsp paprika
- ¼ tsp crushed red pepper flakes

1. Take your food processor and add garlic, yogurt, salt, oil and blend as well.
2. Take a mixing bowl and add chicken, red pepper flakes, paprika, cumin, parsley, garlic, and mix well.
3. Let it marinate for 2-4 hours.
4. Pre-heat Ninja Foodi by pressing the "ROAST" option and setting it to "400 degrees F" and timer to 23 minutes.
5. Let it pre-heat until you hear a beep.
6. Arrange chicken directly inside your cooking pot and lock lid, cook for 15 minutes, flip and cook for the remaining time.

PER SERVING

Calories: 321 | Carbohydrates: 6 g | Protein: 21 g | Fat: 24 g | Sodium: 602 mg | Fiber: 2 g

Printed in Great Britain
by Amazon

DEBORAH H. MOORE

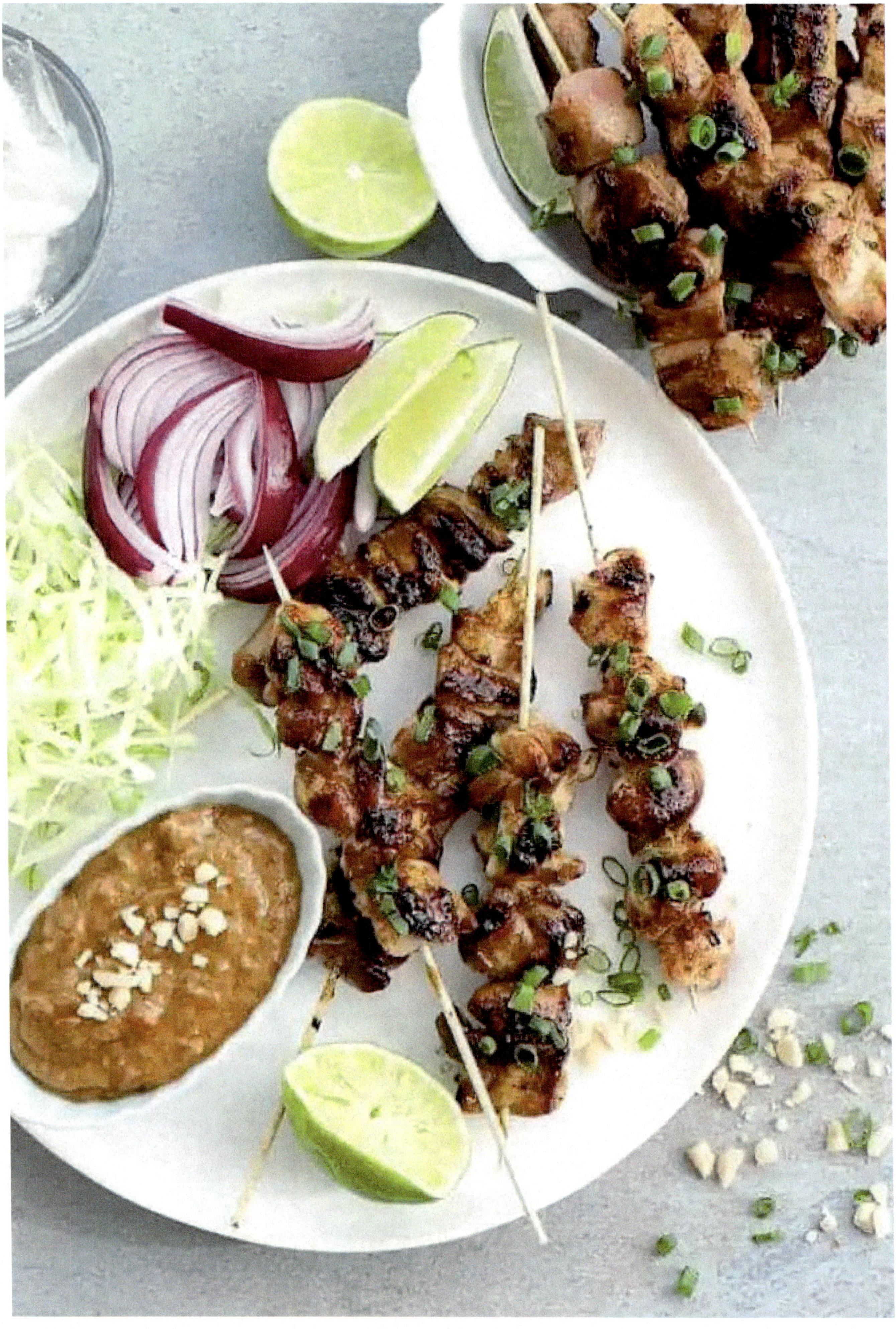

N

nutritional yeast 5

O

olive oil 5, 12, 13, 14, 50, 51, 52, 53
onion 5, 50, 51
onion powder 8
oregano 5, 8, 10, 50

P

panatoes 50, 52
paprika 5, 15, 52
Parmesan cheese 51, 53
parsley 6, 52
pesto 52
pink Himalayan salt 5, 7, 8, 11
pizza dough 50, 53
pizza sauce 50
plain coconut yogurt 6
plain Greek yogurt 5
porcini powder 53
potato 53

R

Ranch dressing 52
raw honey 9, 12, 13
red pepper flakes 5, 8, 14, 15, 51, 53
ricotta cheese 53

S

saffron 52
Serrano pepper 53
sugar 10
summer squash 51

T

tahini 5, 8, 9, 11
thyme 50
toasted almonds 14
tomato 5, 50, 52, 53
turmeric 15

U

unsalted butter 50
unsweetened almond milk 5

V

vegetable broth 50
vegetable stock 51

W

white wine 8, 11
wine vinegar 8, 10, 11

Y

yogurt 5, 6

Z

zucchini 50, 51, 52, 53

Appendix 3 Index

A

all-purpose flour 50, 53
allspice 15
almond 5, 14
ancho chile 10
ancho chile powder 5
apple 9
apple cider vinegar 9
arugula 51
avocado 11

B

bacon 52
balsamic vinegar 7, 12, 52
basil 5, 8, 11, 13
beet 52
bell pepper 50, 51, 53
black beans 50, 51
broccoli 51, 52, 53
buns 52
butter 50

C

canola oil 50, 51, 52
carrot 52, 53
cauliflower 5, 52
cayenne 5, 52
cayenne pepper 52
Cheddar cheese 52
chicken 6
chili powder 50, 51
chipanle pepper 50
chives 5, 6, 52
cinnamon 15
coconut 6
Colby Jack cheese 51
coriander 52
corn 50, 51
corn kernels 50
cumin 5, 10, 15, 50, 51, 52

D

diced panatoes 50
Dijon mustard 7, 12, 13, 51
dry onion powder 52

E

egg 14, 50, 53
enchilada sauce 51

F

fennel seed 53
flour 50, 53
fresh chives 5, 6, 52
fresh cilantro 52
fresh cilantro leaves 52
fresh dill 5
fresh parsley 6, 52
fresh parsley leaves 52

G

garlic 5, 9, 10, 11, 13, 14, 50, 51, 52, 53
garlic powder 8, 9, 52, 53

H

half-and-half 50
hemp seeds 8
honey 9, 51

I

instant rice 51

K

kale 14
kale leaves 14
ketchup 53
kosher salt 5, 10, 15

L

lemon 5, 6, 14, 51, 53
lemon juice 6, 8, 11, 13, 14, 51
lime 9, 12
lime juice 9, 12
lime zest 9, 12

M

maple syrup 7, 12, 53
Marinara Sauce 5
micro greens 52
milk 5, 50
mixed berries 12
Mozzarella 50, 53
Mozzarella cheese 50, 53
mushroom 51, 52
mustard 51, 53
mustard powder 53

Appendix 2 The Dirty Dozen and Clean Fifteen

The Environmental Working Group (EWG) is a nonprofit, nonpartisan organization dedicated to protecting human health and the environment Its mission is to empower people to live healthier lives in a healthier environment. This organization publishes an annual list of the twelve kinds of produce, in sequence, that have the highest amount of pesticide residue-the Dirty Dozen-as well as a list of the fifteen kinds of produce that have the least amount of pesticide residue-the Clean Fifteen.

THE DIRTY DOZEN	
The 2016 Dirty Dozen includes the following produce. These are considered among the year's most important produce to buy organic:	
Strawberries	Spinach
Apples	Tomatoes
Nectarines	Bell peppers
Peaches	Cherry tomatoes
Celery	Cucumbers
Grapes	Kale/collard greens
Cherries	Hot peppers
The Dirty Dozen list contains two additional items kale/collard greens and hot peppers-because they tend to contain trace levels of highly hazardous pesticides.	

THE CLEAN FIFTEEN	
The least critical to buy organically are the Clean Fifteen list. The following are on the 2016 list:	
Avocados	Papayas
Corn	Kiw
Pineapples	Eggplant
Cabbage	Honeydew
Sweet peas	Grapefruit
Onions	Cantaloupe
Asparagus	Cauliflower
Mangos	
Some of the sweet corn sold in the United States are made from genetically engineered (GE) seedstock. Buy organic varieties of these crops to avoid GE produce.	

Appendix 1 Measurement Conversion Chart

Volume Equivalents (Dry)	
US STANDARD	METRIC (APPROXIMATE)
1/8 teaspoon	0.5 mL
1/4 teaspoon	1 mL
1/2 teaspoon	2 mL
3/4 teaspoon	4 mL
1 teaspoon	5 mL
1 tablespoon	15 mL
1/4 cup	59 mL
1/2 cup	118 mL
3/4 cup	177 mL
1 cup	235 mL
2 cups	475 mL
3 cups	700 mL
4 cups	1 L

Volume Equivalents (Liquid)		
US STANDARD	US STANDARD (OUNCES)	METRIC (APPROXIMATE)
2 tablespoons	1 fl.oz.	30 mL
1/4 cup	2 fl.oz.	60 mL
1/2 cup	4 fl.oz.	120 mL
1 cup	8 fl.oz.	240 mL
1 1/2 cup	12 fl.oz.	355 mL
2 cups or 1 pint	16 fl.oz.	475 mL
4 cups or 1 quart	32 fl.oz.	1 L
1 gallon	128 fl.oz.	4 L

Temperatures Equivalents	
FAHRENHEIT(F)	CELSIUS(C) APPROXIMATE)
225 °F	107 °C
250 °F	120 ° °C
275 °F	135 °C
300 °F	150 °C
325 °F	160 °C
350 °F	180 °C
375 °F	190 °C
400 °F	205 °C
425 °F	220 °C
450 °F	235 °C
475 °F	245 °C
500 °F	260 °C

Weight Equivalents	
US STANDARD	METRIC (APPROXIMATE)
1 ounce	28 g
2 ounces	57 g
5 ounces	142 g
10 ounces	284 g
15 ounces	425 g
16 ounces (1 pound)	455 g
1.5 pounds	680 g
2 pounds	907 g